New American STREAMLINE

BERNARD HARTLEY & PETER VINEY

DESTINATIONS

An intensive American English series for advanced students
Workbook A
Units 1–40
REVISED BY IRENE FRANKEL

Oxford University Press

Oxford University Press

198 Madison Avenue
New York, NY 10016 USA

Walton Street
Oxford OX2 6DP England

OXFORD is a trademark of Oxford University Press.

ISBN 0-19-434834-2

Based on the American adaptation by Flamm/Northam
Authors and Publishers Services, Inc.

Editorial Manager: Susan Lanzano
Project Manager: Ken Mencz
Editor: Shirley Brod
Associate Production Editor: Annmarie Lockhart
Picture Researcher: Paul Hahn
Production Manager: Abram Hall
Design by: Design Five

Cover illustration by: Pete Kelly

Illustrations and realia by:
Ray Alma, Alex Bloch, Carlos Castellanos,
Gary Hallgren, Veronica Jones, Tom Powers, Justin
Waldstein, Nina Wallace

The publishers would like to thank the following
for their permission to reproduce photographs:
International Stock

Printing (last digit) 10 9 8 7 6 5 4 3 2 1

Printed in Canada.

TO THE TEACHER

Workbook A of *New American Streamline: Destinations* consists of forty units. Each unit relates directly to the corresponding unit in *New American Streamline: Destinations Units 1–40.*

The *Workbook* is an optional component of the series, designed to provide language summaries and additional written exercises. It may be used in the following ways:

1. In more extensive courses as additional classroom material, providing extra oral practice and written reinforcement and consolidation of the basic core material in the Student Book.
2. As homework material in more intensive situations.

The *Workbook* should only be used after full oral practice of the corresponding unit in the Student Book. The language summaries provide material for review.

Another workbook is available for Units 41–80 of the Student Book, under the title *Workbook B.*

Bernard Hartley
Peter Viney
Irene Frankel

Language Summary

Greetings

Formal
A: *Good morning/afternoon/evening.*
B: *Good morning, etc.*

Formal, on being introduced
A: *How do you do?*
B: *How do you do?*

Polite, friendly
A: *Hello. How are you?*
B: *Very well, thanks, and you?*
A: *I'm fine, thanks.*

Familiar, casual
A: *Hi!*
B: *Hi!*
A: *How are things?/How are you doing?/How are you getting along?*
B: *All right./OK./Not bad.*

Introductions

I'd like you to meet…/May I introduce…?/Hello, I'm….

Thanks and accepting thanks

A: *Thanks./Thank you./Thank you for coming to meet me.*
B: *That's all right./Not at all.*

Polite inquiries and responses

A: *How's work/the family?*
B: *All right./OK./Fine.*
A: *Did you have a good trip?*

Apologies

Sorry./I'm so sorry.
I'm afraid not.

Exercise

A: ....
B: ....
A: ....
B: ....

A: ....
B: ....
A: ....
B: ....

A: ....
B: ....
A: ....
B: ....

A: ....
B: ....
C: ....

A: ....
B: ....
A: ....
B: ....

A: ....
B: ....
A: ....
B: ....

A: ....
B: ....
A: ....
B: ....

Look at the pictures. Read all the sentences carefully and use them in the blanks above to make conversations.
Use each sentence only once.

A: Oh, I'm so sorry!
A: Jeanette! Hello! How are you?
B: How do you do, Charlie?
B: Nice to meet you, Tom.
A: Hi! Can I have your autograph?
B: Yes, thanks. And thanks for coming to meet me.
B: I'm afraid not. Sorry.

A: They're all OK. Do you have time for a quick drink?
A: Good morning, Janet.
B: Fine. How are you?
A: Dad, this is Charlie Grunt.
B: Yes, sure.
A: Hello, Mike. I haven't seen you for ages.
B: Excuse me?

B: That's all right. It wasn't your fault.
A: I'm all right. Did you have a good flight?
B: Good morning, Jim.
A: Aren't you Cliff Black?
C: How do you do, sir?
B: Hello, Peter. How's the family?
A: I'd like you to meet Tom Garcia. He's our new sales representative.

Unit 2

Language Summary

I, He, She, It, We, You, They	'll will won't will not	be doing that	at 6:00. from 6 to 7. during the program. for 10 minutes.

The flight <u>leaves</u> at 8:30.

<u>I'm meeting</u> him tomorrow.

<u>We'll begin</u> at about 6:30.

Exercise 1

A: When does the next flight to New York leave?
B: At eight forty-five.
A: And at what time does it get there?
B: At eleven-oh-five. It takes two hours and twenty minutes.

Look at the schedules.
Practice four more conversations like this.

	From	To	Depart	Arrive
Flight	Chicago, IL	New York, NY	8:45 AM	11:05 AM
Bus	San Francisco, CA	Los Angeles, CA	8:15 AM	4:20 AM
Train	Washington, DC	New Orleans, LA	6:00 AM	11:30 PM
Ferry	New London, CT	Block Island, RI	5:00 PM	7:15 PM
Helicopter	Kennedy Airport, NYC	LaGuardia Airport, NYC	1:15 PM	1:25 PM

Exercise 2

Kay Gordon is playing golf this evening. She's meeting Tom Harris at 5:00. They'll drive to the golf course, and they'll start playing at about 5:30. They'll probably finish at 8:30. They'll be playing golf from 5:30 to 8:30.

Use these words and write a similar paragraph: John Silva / tennis / Linda Lee / 5:30 / walk / tennis court / begin / 5:45 / finish / 7:00

Exercise 3

Kay Gordon is the manager of an insurance company. This is her calendar for tomorrow.

She's meeting Stu Granger at 9:15.

Write five more sentences.

1. ....
   ....

2. ....
   ....

3. ....
   ....

5 Thursday

9:15 - Meet Stu Granger (new accountant)

10:30 - Interview Les Turner (for admin. ass't. position)

11:00 - Visit Catalina Street branch office

1:00 - Lunch, Laura Stanton (Continental Computers)

3:00 - See Jim Palmer (Western Stationery)

6:00 - Golf, Tom Harris

4. ....
   ....

5. ....

Exercise 4

George Townsend is a fashion buyer for a large department store in Chicago. Tomorrow he's flying to New York on business. This is his calendar.

8:30 AM *What'll he be doing at 8:30 in the morning?*
         He'll be waiting for his flight at O'Hare Airport.

Write questions and answers for: 10:00 AM / 11:45 AM / 3:00 PM / 6:00 PM / 8:30 PM

10:00 AM ....

....

12:00 noon ....

....

3:00 PM ....

....

New York via World
Airlines - depart O'Hare
Airport 8:45, arrive NY
11:05 - check in by 8:15 a.m.
Hotel Palace, Madison
Avenue at 50th, check in
by 6:00 p.m.

2:00 - 5:00 Carolyn Roth,
Mode, Inc. - new contract?
5:30 Attend Calvin Pines
fashion show, Hilton Hotel
8:30 Dinner - Dinah von
Burstenburg - Four Seasons

6:00 PM ....

....

8:30 PM ....

....

Unit 3

Language Summary

Name   *What's your name? I'm/My name's (William Paine).*

Date and Place of Birth   *When/Where were you born? I was born on July second/in (Providence, RI).*

Nationality   *Where are you from? I'm (American)./I'm from (the United States).*

Marital Status   *Are you married? Yes, I am./No, I'm not. I'm single.*

Address   *What's your address? I live at/My address is (77 Sunshine Boulevard, Hollywood, California).*

Education   *Where did you go to school/college? I went to (Whitney High School/Yale University School of Drama).*

Profession   *What do you do? I'm an (actor)./I work in (show business).*

Exercise 1

Last Name	....	....	....
First and Middle Names	....	....	....
Date of Birth	....	....	....
Place of Birth	....	....	....
Nationality	....	....	....
Address	....	....	....
	....	....	....
Education	....	....	....
	....	....	....
Profession	....	....	....
Marital Status	....	....	....

Read these three texts and complete the forms above.

" *My name's Rita…Rita Luisa Colon. Now, what can I tell you about myself? Let's see. I was born on March 23rd — I'd prefer not to tell you the year! Los Angeles is my hometown. I was brought up and went to school there — Beverly Hills High, then on to UCLA. I graduated with a degree in drama. I got married in 1988 when I was only 22, but it broke up after a couple of years. I was really glad I never changed my name. I've been very lucky in my career as an actress. I still live in L.A. I have an apartment in the San Andreas Towers on Sunset Drive.* "

" I was named Irwin Stanley after my grandfather, Irwin Stanley Theissen, who had been, among other things, the mayor of Cranston, Rhode Island. I've been a teacher all my life in different parts of the state. I now teach at Cranston High School, where I went to school myself before going on to Brown University to study English. I'm a widower now. My wife died three years ago, and I live with my eldest daughter at 26 Poplar Avenue in Cranston, which is only a stone's throw from where I was born in 1934 on April 25th. "

Exercise 2

1. Interview a classmate and write a short biography of him or her.

2. Write a short autobiography.

LANCASTER COUNTY, PA   June 6
WEEKLY BUGLE

BENNETT OFF TO CALIFORNIA

Jean Bennett, who was in town visiting her parents, Elliot and Katherine Bennett, for her birthday yesterday, is off to California, where she'll be working in a national park as a forest ranger. Twenty-two-year-old Jean attended the Carnegie Academy and the University of Pennsylvania. Jean, whose parents still live in the house at 472 Glencoe Road where Jean was born, is engaged to Dr. George Sullivan, a dentist. Her parents expect the couple to have their wedding here in Millersville some time next year.

Unit 4

Language Summary

| She's / They've | been doing that | for 2 hours. / since 6 o'clock. |
| | done (a lot). | |

| How | long | have they / has she | been doing that? |
| | much / many | | done? |

What will she be doing tomorrow?
She'll be doing (this).

| How | much / many | will | she / they | have done? |

| She / They | 'll / will | have done (a lot). |

big/bigger/biggest … as big as …
economical/more economical/the most economical

Exercise 1

How many cars were they making per week in January? 600.
Ask and answer for the other months on the graph.

1. ....
2. ....
3. ....
4. ....
5. ....
6. ....

Exercise 2

Look at the graph.

They made 2,400 cars in January, 3,000 in February, and 3,200 in March. So they have made 8,600 cars.

How many will they have made by the end of April?
They'll have made 12,000.

Ask and answer for May, June, and July.

1. ....
....

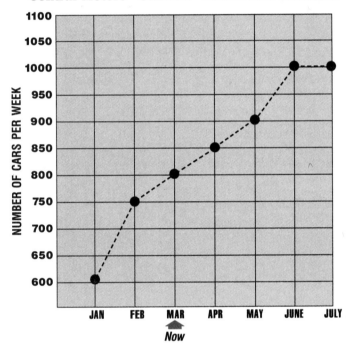

Central Motors "Stallion" Production Schedule

NUMBER OF CARS PER WEEK — JAN FEB MAR APR MAY JUNE JULY
Now

2. ....
....

3. ....
....

Exercise 3

David and Andrea Arlotta got married two years ago. They want to buy a house. They've both been working overtime, and they are able to save $400 a month. They started saving exactly one year ago today, July 1. They need $12,000 as a 15% down payment. Write full answers.

How long have they been married? *They've been married for two years.*

1. How long have they been saving? ....
2. How much do they save monthly? ....
3. How much have they already saved? ....
4. How much will they have saved by December? ....
5. Will they have saved enough by next June? ....
6. When will they have saved enough? ....

Unit 5

Language Summary

| I | enjoy
love
like
don't like
dislike
can't stand
hate | doing this. | I'm | afraid of
terrified of
frightened of
scared of
tired of
bored with
fed up with
interested in | doing that. | I | began
started
stopped
gave up | doing this. |

Exercise

Look at this:

football
> I like playing football.
> My brother started playing football at school.
> Some of my coworkers are bored with hearing about football.
> My friends aren't interested in watching football on TV.
> I began reading about Australian football.

or something else…

Now select one of the verbs from the Language Summary and make a sentence using an *-ing* form with each of these words.

1. house..

....

2. bed..

....

3. job...

....

4. friends...

....

5. crowded airports..

....

6. adventure stories...

....

7. self-service cafeterias..

....

8. the beach..

....

9. classical music ....

....

10. money ....

....

11. spare time..

....

12. on vacation ....

....

13. supermarket...

....

14. cars...

....

15. children..

....

16. homework...

....

17. English...

....

18. television commercials ....

....

19. horror movies ....

....

20. arguments..

....

21. important people..

....

22. TV quiz shows...

....

23. presents...

....

24. alarm clock ....

....

Unit 6

Look at this:

Business Letters

Salutations
When writing to an individual who is...   **For example**

Someone with whom you are on a first-name basis, you can
use the person's first name.

Mr. Robin Brown
Dear Robin:

A man you don't know, use the title *Mr.*

Mr. Victor Semple
Dear Mr. Semple:

A woman you don't know, use the title *Ms.*[1]

Ms. Sherry Greenspan
Dear Ms. Greenspan:

A person you don't know whose gender is not clear from the name, use the
person's full name.

Terry Murphy
Dear Terry Murphy:

When writing to an organization and you don't know the name or
title of the recipient... [2]   **For example**

In formal correspondence, use a general salutation.[3]

Dear Sir or Madam:
or
Dear Madam or Sir:

In informal or routine correspondence, you can instead use the name of the
organization or the name of the department.

Dear PhotoMart:
Dear Parts Manager:

Complimentary Closings

Formal

Sincerely yours,

Less Formal

Sincerely,

Informal

Regards,
Best regards,

Notes

1. If, however, the woman has expressed a preference for
   Mrs. or *Miss,* honor her preference.

2. If you know the recipient's name but use an *Attention*
   line, you should use *Dear Sir* or *Madam,* since
   technically you are writing to the organization,
   not the individual.

For this reason, it's better to avoid the *Attention* line.
   Western Insurance Co.
   32 Meadowlands Parkway
   Secaucus, NJ 07601
   Attention: Mr. Victor Semple
   Dear Sir or Madam:

3. If possible, find out the name and title of the recipient.

Exercise 1

Imagine that you are being interviewed by a career counselor
at a state Jobs Service office. Complete the conversation.

Counselor: Hello. My name is Lee Hanover. Please have
a seat.

You: ....

Counselor: First, what about qualifications...or...special
skills?

You: ....

Counselor: I see. And where did you go to school?

You: ....

Counselor: What was your major and what were your
favorite courses?

You: ....

Counselor: And which ones did you get the best grades in?

You: ....

Counselor: What subjects did you like least?

You: ....

Counselor: Why?

You: ....

Counselor: I understand. And what about your leisure
activities...what do you like to do in your
spare time?

You: ....

Counselor: That's interesting. Now, what kind of job do
you want to do?

You: ....

Counselor: Why do you think you'd like doing that?

You: ....

Counselor: Well, let me see what we have in our
computer bank.

Look at this:

KINDERGARTEN TEACHER for elementary school in Mandanga. All teaching in English, U.S. curriculum followed. Candidates must have teaching certification and Master's degree. Experience in kindergarten teaching preferred. Previous overseas living an advantage. Write with brief details of qualifications to: Mr. Arnold Benedict, International Teaching Inc., 1221 Vauxhall Drive, Brooklyn, NY 11201.

Exercise 3

Look at the ad, the résumé, and the cover letter.

Alexander D. O'Hare
1289 Glenwood Drive
Petaluma, CA 94952
(707) 778-7072

Experience
1993-95   Work-study experience at Petaluma
            Community College
            Assisted in Financial Aid office;
            answered phones; helped students
            complete forms; answered students'
            questions; occasionally typed letters
            and memos for Director; filed records.

Computer Skills
            Experienced with IBM PC, Apple
            Macintosh, and Power PC
            Proficient in WordPerfect, LotusNotes,
            Pagemaker, and Filemaker

Education
            A.A. Petaluma Community College,
            Computer Studies, 1995

References available upon request.

Look at these two ads. Reply to one of them or to a job you would like. Write out your résumé, a cover letter, and the envelope.

Here is a reply to the ad. Write it out using correct form and punctuation.

340 beacon street boston ma 02106 march 7 1995 mr arnold benedict international teaching inc 1221 vauxhall drive brooklyn ny 11201 dear mr benedict i saw your ad for a kindergarten teaching position in this months issue of teacher magazine and I would like to be considered for the position i have a masters degree from northeastern university in elementary education with an emphasis on teaching younger children in 1992 and 1993 i taught first grade at the american school in guayaquil ecuador and since then ive been teaching kindergarten in the public schools of boston i have several friends from mandanga and i know i would feel at home there i have enclosed my résumé and a letter of recommendation from the principal in guayaquil i can be reached at 617-555-8372. i look forward to hearing from you sincerely yours patricia biaggi enclosures

Administrative Assistant
Entry level position. M–F 9–5:30. Small architectural company seeks detail-oriented assistant with good social, math, & phone skills. PC experience a plus. Send résumé to Box 342, Evening Post, Petaluma, CA 94950.

1289 Glenwood Drive
Petaluma, CA 94952
June 4, 1995

Box 342
Evening Post
Petaluma, CA 94950

Dear Sir or Madam:

I am applying for the position of Administrative Assistant advertised on Sunday, June 4, 1995.

I have just graduated with my Associate's degree in computer studies from Petaluma Community College. During my two years there, I was a work-study student in the Financial Aid office and gained a great deal of experience working with people in an office setting.

I would appreciate the opportunity to discuss my qualifications with you. You can reach me at (707) 778-7072.

Sincerely yours,

Alexander D. O'Hare
Alexander D. O'Hare

Sales Consultant
Major department store in fashionable mall needs sales consultants in various departments: electronics, jewelry, books & games, clothing, accessories. Send résumé to Personnel Dept., J.C. Nichols, Century Plaza Mall, Aspen Road, West Orange, NJ 07052.

Office Assistant
Real Estate office
Ability to handle busy phones, good in math, must work under pressure. H.S. grad, some experience. Apply, with résumé, to Rosenthal & Rosenthal, 1451 41st Street, New Hyde Park, NY 11010.

Unit 7

Language Summary

hope to (do)	*want to (do)*	*manage to (do)*	*threaten to (do)*
refuse to (do)	*would like to (do)*	*decide to (do)*	*have to (do)*
plan to (do)	*intend to (do)*	*demand to (do)*	*be going to (do)*
offer to (do)	*expect to (do)*	*need to (do)*	
agree to (do)	*promise to (do)*	*arrange to (do)*	

Exercise

Bank Crisis
"NO COMMENT" was all the president of Second Southern Bank would say this morning. The bank closed its doors at noon on Tuesday and has not opened since.

(refuse) *The president refused to comment.*

Continue.

Fighter Crashes
AN F-42 FIGHTER plane has crashed. It happened over the Gulf of Mexico near Pensacola this morning. The pilot escaped unhurt. He ejected two miles off the coast and was picked up by a Coast Guard helicopter.

1. (manage) ....

....

Daryll Walker Unhappy
L.A. DODGERS' MANAGER Tony La Bruno admitted today that he had received a trade request from star pitcher Daryll Walker. Walker has been unhappy with La Bruno and the Dodgers for some time and feels that he would be happier on a new team.

6. (would like)...

....

Factory Sit-in
FACTORY WORKERS at Darnley Chemical Corporation's Pittsfield plant are continuing their sit-in protest against management's plans to shut the plant down. A spokesperson for the workers said, "We shall not be moved."

2. (refuse)..

....

July Summit
IT WAS ANNOUNCED today that world leaders would meet at the United Nations in July. There had been some disagreement about the time and place, but these problems have now been solved.

7. (agree)...

....

Tax Cuts on the Way
THERE WILL be tax reductions in the next fiscal year. "We will not break our word to the people who voted for us in the last election," the President stated at a banquet in Denver last night.

3. (promise)..

....

New City Hall for Bradyville
THE BRADYVILLE CITY COUNCIL voted 7–2 in favor of a new city hall last night. The decision came after months of discussion. Construction will begin next spring and will cost $3 million.

8. (decide) ....

....

Olympic Gold?
MARY DEXTER, the American 400-meter champion, ran her fastest time this year in Boston last night. After the race, Dexter commented, "Now for the Olympics. Only the gold will be good enough for me."

4. (hope)..

....

Pasta Maker to Go?
BUONI PASTA, the largest producer of pasta and macaroni products on the East Coast, is considering relocating its giant pasta plant to the South. Buoni officials said the low taxes in the South were its main reasons for moving, and that they would stay here if the city made them an offer they couldn't refuse.

9. (threaten) ....

....

Hospital Workers Offered 5%
AN INCREASE of 5% is the latest pay offer to workers in the city's two hospitals. The mayor says that this is the final offer, but union leaders will probably press for further negotiations.

5. (offer)..

....

Texxo Takeover
TEXAS MULTIMILLIONAIRE Maggie Silver announced today that she has offered to buy a 20% share of the Texxo Corporation. Asked about Silver's proposal to take over Texxo Corp., Texxo Chair Thomas B. Worthington had no comment.

10. (intend)..

....

Unit 8

Language Summary

I	'm	delighted to (hear) …	It	is	wonderful to (hear) …	Love,
	was	willing to (help) …		was	nice to (know) …	Lots of love,
He	is	sorry to (lose) …		will be	hard to (know) …	All my love,
She	was	happy to (gain) …		has been	great to (be) …	Best wishes,
We	are	sad to (read) …			interesting to (look at) …	Warm regards,
You	were	ready to (help) …				
They		surprised to (find out) …				
		upset to (learn) …				

Exercise 1

I heard about all your problems. I was very sorry.
I was very sorry to hear about your problems.

Continue.

1. Do you need any help? You know I'm always available.

....

2. It was great! We got away to Florida for two weeks.

....

3. I read in the paper about the birth of your son, and I was really delighted.

....

4. We visited the Museum of Modern Art in New York. It was fascinating.

....

5. We found out about your accident yesterday. All of us were upset.

....

6. Going back to school after the summer is hard.

....

7. We got your pictures in the mail today. We were very happy.

....

8. The doctor is ready. She will see you now.

....

9. What fun! I saw all my friends from school again at our 10th reunion.

....

10. I was surprised when I saw you on TV last night.

....

11. I'm sorry, but I have to say that this work isn't good enough.

....

12. It's wonderful. You have such a close family.

....

continued

Exercise 2

A: Guess what! Nancy and Dwight are getting married!
B: That's great! *I'm delighted to hear that.*

Continue. Use a different adjective + infinitive for each one.

1. A: Have you heard? Ken was promoted!

   B: Terrific! ....

2. A: I just spoke to Lillian. Her mother is doing much better.

   B: What good news! ....

3. A: Justin won't be in today. His grandfather died.

   B: That's too bad. ....

4. A: I just found out that Barbara got a new job.

   B: Really? ....

Exercise 3

Look at this:

SAN JOSE. **Almeria.** - Serie 92, n. °62
Playa de los Genoveses
Plage des "Genoveses"
"Genoveses" Beach
Strand der "Genoveses"

Dear Abe and Rachel,
      Here we are in sunny Spain! It's great to have dry, warm weather every day. We're being very lazy, but sometimes it's nice just to lie on the beach doing nothing.
      Dave was surprised to find that people could understand his Spanish! It was hard to go to all those night classes last winter, but now he's delighted to be able to use what he learned. That's all for now - back to the beach!

See you soon!
   Love,
      Sharon and Dave

ARTAMA / Almeria
Prohibida la reproduc reproduccion - Depósito Legal

A

Mr. and Mrs. Abe Weinstein

275 Carlton Terrace

Milwaukee, Wisconsin 53210

U.S.A.

Impresión: Casamaió Barcelona

John and Ellen Ross are on vacation in London. Use these cues and write a card to their friend Pam Barnes in Dallas. She lives at 1134 Westfork Boulevard, Dallas, Texas 75225.

interesting/museums and palaces/surprised/discover/hotel prices/very high/not hard/get around London/great/the Queen/Buckingham Palace/happy/you again/next week/pleased/you willing/us/at the airport/nice/home/warm regards

Exercise 4

Imagine that you are on vacation in a faraway part of your country or in a foreign country. Choose a place, and write a postcard to some friends at home.

Unit 9

Someone	advised	me	to (do)	something.
	allowed	you		
	encouraged	him		
	expected	her		
	forbade	us		
	forced	them		
	helped	David		
	invited	the children		
	persuaded			
	preferred			
	reminded			
	told			
	wanted			
It	embarrassed			

I'm (not)	here	to	do that.
	there		listen.
			give an opinion.

He's too	young	to (do) that.
	tired	

We seem to have fights all the time.

Exercise 1

"If I were you, Mrs. Torres, I'd take traveler's checks," said the bank manager.

(advise) *The bank manager advised her to take traveler's checks.*

Continue.

1. "Don't forget to fasten your seat belts," the flight attendant said.

(remind) ....

....

2. "Excuse me. Can you get that book down for me, please?" asked the little boy. "Sure. I'll help you," the librarian replied.

(help) ....

....

3. "Would you like to see my paintings, Judy?" he asked.

(invite) ....

....

4. "Take biology this semester, Sandra, and physics next semester," the guidance counselor said.

(advise) ....

....

5. "You have to play well today, guys," the coach said. "It's the most important game of the season."

(want) ....

....

6. "Business should improve soon," the economist predicted.

(expect) ....

....

7. "Go away, all of you!" he shouted. "Leave me alone!"

(tell) ....

....

8. "You can't come into the store barefoot, buddy," the guard said.

(not allow) ....

....

9. "Don't come home late," Bill's father said.

(forbid)..

....

10. "Can I have dinner at Jan's house, Mom?," asked Suzy. "I really think you should eat at home tonight. I've cooked your favorite dinner."

(prefer)..

....

11. "Don't be too disappointed, Robert. You can take the test again," the driving instructor said.

(encourage)..

....

12. "Don't argue. Just follow that car!" the police officer ordered the taxi driver. "All right, all right," she replied.

(force)..

....

13. "I'd rather not go there." "Oh, come on, Sam, you have to." "No...really." "Oh, come on." "Oh...all right. I'll go."

(persuade) ....

....

14. "I didn't want to do that. It was so embarrassing... but I had to," he said.

(embarrass) ....

....

continued

excited   *He was too excited to speak.*

Continue.

He was speechless when he heard he had won.

1. She can't take her vacation now. She has too much work to do.

(busy) ....

....

2. The kids have to stay home from school. They both have fevers.

(sick) ....

....

3. He was so tired that he couldn't eat dinner.

(exhausted) ....

....

4. They couldn't move because they were so frightened.

(terrified) ....

....

Unit 10

Language Summary

He went somewhere to do something.
I'll make the arrangements.

Exercise 1

Fill in the blanks with the appropriate forms of
do and *make*.

Stan Slade—Private Eye

My name's Slade, Stan Slade, private investigator. The story begins one Saturday morning in January. I hadn't been very busy. In fact, I hadn't had any jobs since Christmas and only one person had called this week to .... an appointment. At about 11:00, this guy came into my office. He looked rich, very rich, indeed—you know, fur coat, fat cigar. He threw $5,000 on the desk.

"That's for one week," he said. "You're working for me."

Well, I don't usually .... $5,000 a month, let alone in a week. "What do you want me to .... ?" I asked. He sat down.

"This is an important job, Slade. I don't want you to .... any mistakes, OK? I want you to .... arrangements to follow my wife. Here's a picture of her. She's much younger than me and, well, I want to know

everything she .... , everything! I want to know what time she gets up, what kinds of exercise she .... , when she .... chores, where she ..... her errands, and who she .... them with. I want every detail. I want to know when she .... a phone call, and who she calls. Can you .... that?"

"Sure," I said. Hey, for $5,000, I could .... almost anything.

"By the way, let me .... a suggestion," said the man.

"Sure, you're paying," I said.

".................... sure she doesn't see you. If I find out she even suspects she's being followed, well, let's just say I could .... a lot of trouble for you."

"She'll never know I'm there. I won't .... a sound."

The man left my office. I looked at the photo he'd given me, and the address. "Well," I thought to myself, "I suppose I'd better go out and .... some work."

Exercise 2

9:00 Got up, made coffee	Drugstore—prescription
9:45 Left house	Hair salon—hair and nails
Post office—stamps	Newsstand—magazine
Coffee shop—made call at	Cleaners—picked up clothes
pay phone	12:32 Returned home

These are some of Slade's notes.
Post office–stamps
She went to the post office to get some stamps.
Write five more sentences like this.

Exercise 3

This is the rest of Slade's story. Fill in the blanks with the appropriate forms of *do* and *make*.

It was pretty boring. I hoped that she would .... something interesting, but nothing happened. On the third day, I parked outside her house as usual. I started .... the crossword puzzle. I heard footsteps. Suddenly, there was a tap on the window. I looked up. It was my old buddy, Lieutenant O'Casey of the 18th Precinct, Los Angeles Police Department.

".................... me a favor, O'Casey," I said. "Go away. I've got a job to ...."

"So have I, Slade," he replied. "A lady has .... a complaint. She says you've been following her. Have you

been trying to .... a date with her or something?"

"OK, OK, O'Casey. I'm working for her husband."

"Don't .... me laugh, Slade! She isn't married. Who's paying you?" I described the rich cigar-smoker. O'Casey laughed. "I suppose he asked you to .... a report on all her movements?"

"Yeah. That's right."

"Well," O'Casey said slowly, "the lady is Laura Van Gelt, the millionaire. You remember, her father .... a fortune in soybeans. Your man sounds like Pete Greenstreet, the international jewel thief!"

Unit 11

Language Summary

Lend me 50 cents.
Close the door, will you?
Do you want some coffee?
Would you like some coffee?

Can I	*ask you something?*
Could I	
May I	
Might I	
Do you mind if I	
I wonder if I could	

Would you mind if I asked you something?

Would you mind doing something?
I wonder if you'd mind doing something?
Would you be kind enough to do something?
Would you be so kind as to do something?
I wonder if you can/could help me?

Would you mind if I did something?

Not at all. No, go right ahead.
I don't mind at all. Please do.
I'm sorry, but I'd rather you didn't.
Thank you so much.
No, thanks. I'm just looking.

Note: When you make a polite request, it is often the way you say something that is important, not the choice of a particular expression. You can say *"I wonder if you'd mind helping me?"* in a rude way, or *"Let me have a quarter"* in a polite and friendly way.

Exercise 1

You're in a hot and stuffy room. You have to keep the door closed.
Would you mind opening a window?

1. Your suitcase is on a luggage rack. It's much too heavy for you to take down.

....

2. You have just answered the phone. There's a pot of soup on the stove, and it's boiling over.

....

3. You're in your office meeting with a very important customer. Your boss comes in to say she must see you for a minute.

....

4. You're at work in an office you share. The air conditioning is on very high, and you feel very cold.

....

Exercise 2

You want to ask someone a sensitive or very delicate question. You can say:

    A. *May I ask you something?*
or **B.** *Do you mind if I ask you something?*
or **C.** *Would you mind if I asked you something?*

Write one question for each of these.

1. You're in an elevator in an office building with a stranger. He's carrying a briefcase you like very much. You want to know where he bought it.

2. There are two computers in your office, but only one has the software you need, and it's on your coworker's desk. Ask if you can use that computer.

3. You're in a restaurant you've been in before. You're looking at the menu, and the prices seem much higher than you remember. Ask the server if the prices are higher.

4. You're thinking of applying for a job in another department, and you've just met someone who works there. Ask how she likes working there.

Exercise 3

1. You're in a store. The salesperson has just said, "Can I help you?" You only came into the store because it's raining. What might you say?

2. You're at a party. You're talking to someone you've just met. He's just said, "Do you mind if I smoke?" What do you say?

3. You're at a friend's house and you have to make a phone call. What do you say?

4. You're with a friend sitting at a table for four at a fast-food restaurant. The only free seats are at your table. Two strangers come over with trays and say, "I wonder if we could sit here." What might you say to them?

Unit 12

Language Summary

I have three more <u>shirts to pack.</u>
Do you have <u>a book to read</u> on the plane?

Is there <u>anywhere to put it</u>?
There's <u>nothing to worry</u> about.

Remember to do…/forget to do…

Exercise 1

Judy Hotdinger has just arrived at the Statler Towers Hotel. She's asking the desk clerk about services in the hotel.

Ms. Hotdinger: Is there *anywhere to get* some toothpaste?
Clerk: Yes, you can get some at the drugstore, over there.

Write four other questions with … *anywhere to* … that she might ask.

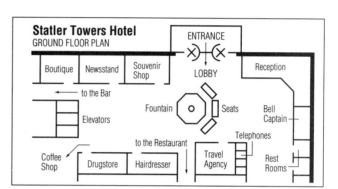

Exercise 2

Haven't you finished packing yet? (three more shirts)
No, I have three more shirts to pack.

1. Have you finished work yet? (several more pages)

....
....

2. Have you done all your homework? (two more exercises)

....
....

3. Haven't you finished that book yet? (four more chapters)

....
....

4. Have you addressed all the envelopes yet? (a few more)

....
....

5. Have you made your car rental and hotel reservations? (one more phone call)

....
....

Exercise 3

The Wilsons are on their first camping trip. They've just unloaded the car, and they see that they've forgotten several important things.
They remembered to bring some cans of food, but they forgot to bring a can opener.
Look at the pictures below and write four more sentences.

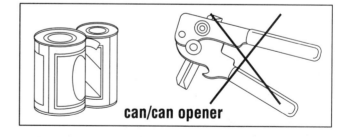

can/can opener

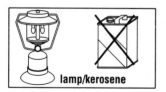

lamp/kerosene

dishes/forks

flashlight/batteries

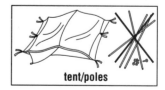

tent/poles

Exercise 4

Robin Caruso is a television news reporter. For her latest documentary "Survival," she's spending two weeks on a desert island with a camera crew. They don't have any food.

They just have these things: an ax/a gun/some fish hooks/some matches/a hammer and nails/a two-way radio/a pen and paper/a magnifying glass/some books/plenty of fresh water/a knife.
They have a two-way radio to use in emergencies.

Write ten more sentences.

Unit 13

Exercise 1

These are some of the signs you might see at or near an airport. Look at the expressions below. Put the correct ones under the signs. The first one has been done for you.

1. *Auto Rental*

2. ....

3. ....

4. ....

5. ....

6. ....

7. ....

8. ....

9. ....

10. ....

11. ....

12. ....

13. ....

14. ....

Information	Baggage Claim	Shuttle Bus	Post Office	Handicapped Facilities
Baggage Carts	Auto Rental	Immigration	Currency Exchange	Airport
Taxis	First Aid	Nursery	Restaurant	

Exercise 2

TO Mexico City, Mexico							
FROM New York, NY/ Newark / NJ, USA							
Freq.	**Depart (EST)**	**Airport**	**Arrive (CST)**	**Airline**	**Eq**	**Meals**	
X6	7:30a	LGA	11:03a				
135	9:10a	JFK	1:00p				
246	11:15a	JFK	4:45p				
X17	2:25p	JFK	6:15p				
17	3:25p	JFK	7:15p				
X46	8:10p	EWR	4:09a				

KEYS

Eq=Equipment

Frequency
1=Monday
2=Tuesday, etc.
X=daily except

EST=Eastern
    Standard Time
CST=Central
    Standard Time

Airports
LGA=LaGuardia
JFK=Kennedy
EWR=Newark

Look at this conversation.

A: Would you mind giving me some information about flights to Mexico City?

B: Not at all. When would you like to travel?

A: This Sunday, if possible.

B: What time of day?

A: As early as possible.

B: OK. There's a flight at 7:30–it gets in at 11:03.

A: Does that go from Kennedy or LaGuardia?

B: LaGuardia.

A: Yes, that would be all right.

Now write a similar conversation for someone who wants to fly late on Thursday.

Exercise 3

Some friends from abroad are coming to your country for a short stay.

Write down five things that you would recommend for them to do.

I'd tell them to rent a car.

Exercise 4

Imagine that you are planning a trip to the United States.

What would you like to see?

What would you expect to eat?

What would you hope to do?

Read this carefully. It is adapted from a booklet produced by the New York Federal Reserve Bank. Use the blank check below, and write out a check to pay the current bill on Diane Crane's U.S. Express credit card. Her card number is 5719-0121-4248-81008, and she owes $147.15. Also fill in the check register.

Know your checks

Check register
This is used for keeping an accurate record of your account. It should be used to record payments, deposits, and fees charged.

Account name
This is the way your branch will identify your account. It should be mentioned together with the account number in any correspondence. Your address can be printed here also. This information provides greater security to the recipient of the check.

Check number
Each check is identified by a number. It should be mentioned in all correspondence about the check.

Check routing number
This identifies your bank when the check is processed manually.

Magnetic coding
A series of numbers is printed in magnetic ink in a format that allows high-speed electronic processing. The numbers include the routing number (sometimes reformatted), followed by the account number, followed by the check number.

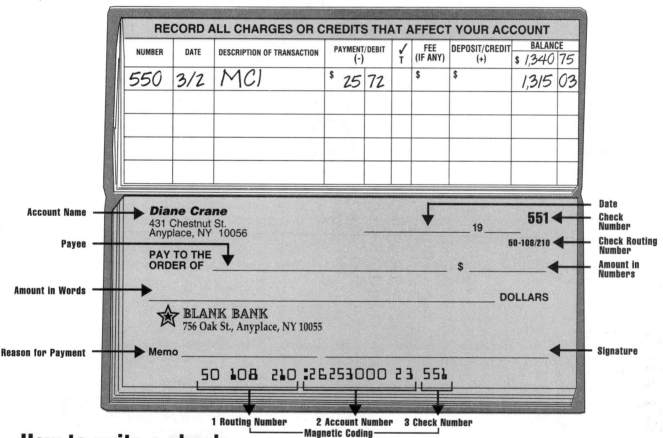

How to write a check

Check register
Fill out the check register when you write the check. This is how you will know what your balance is and who you have paid.

Date
Write the full date of the day you write the check. Note: In the United States, the date is written in month-day-year order.

Payee
Write the name of the party to whom you are making payment here, after "PAY TO THE ORDER OF." If you are withdrawing cash from your account, write "Cash" in this space.

Amount in numbers
Write as close to the dollar sign ($) as possible. The acceptable alternative versions are shown below:

$\$12.50 \quad \$12\frac{50}{}$

Amount in words
Start as far to the left as possible. Make sure that no blanks are left in the check for fraudulent additions. Draw a line from the end of the last word to the word "Dollars." Make sure the words match the amount in numbers. Remember to use hyphens in numbers from 21 to 99. The acceptable versions are given below:

Twelve and $\frac{50}{100}$

Twenty-one and $\frac{xx}{100}$

Reason for payment
Next to "Memo," write the number of the invoice you are paying, the number of your account if you are paying a credit card bill, or a note for using the check as a receipt.

Signature
This should match the signature filed at the bank when you opened your checking account.

continued

Find words in the text that mean:

1. a person who receives something

2. something extra

3. the local office of a large organization

4. a bill

5. record of checks kept by the sender

6. unfilled space

7. exchange of letters

8. person's name written by him/herself

9. the amount of money you have in the bank

10. person to whom something is paid

Exercise 3

What do you think these sentences mean?

1. "Your address on the check provides greater security to the recipient of the check."

☐ **A.** The payee will receive the check more quickly.

☐ **B.** The bank will be nicer to the payee.

☐ **C.** The payee will be protected better.

2. "Make sure that no blanks are left for fraudulent additions."

☐ **A.** If you leave a blank, someone may dishonestly write in words to increase the amount.

☐ **B.** If you leave a blank, the bank may make mistakes when adding it up.

☐ **C.** If you leave a blank, the payee may think you want to cheat him/her.

3. "This should match the signature filed at the bank when you opened your checking account."

☐ **A.** When you sign a check, always write your signature in the same place.

☐ **B.** When you sign a check, your signature should be the same as the one you gave to the bank.

☐ **C.** When you sign a check, you should use the same color ink as in the signature you gave to the bank.

4. "A series of numbers is printed in magnetic ink in a format that allows high-speed electronic processing."

☐ **A.** These numbers are written in a way that can be read by computers.

☐ **B.** These numbers are written in a way that lets them be read quickly.

☐ **C.** These numbers are written in a way that allows the check to be made out properly.

Exercise 4

Look at the check on the previous page. Diane Crane wants to make a deposit to her account. She has a check for $123.00, another for $45.00, and $102.00 in cash. Fill it out for her. Then fill in the check register.

				DOLLARS	CENTS
CHECKING ACCOUNT DEPOSIT TICKET	Please be sure all items are properly endorsed. List checks separately. FOR CLEAR COPY PRESS FIRMLY WITH BALL POINT PEN	☆ **BLANK BANK** 756 Oak St., Anyplace, NY 10055 **CHECKING ACCOUNT DEPOSIT TICKET**	CASH		
			CHECKS		
		DATE / ITEM COUNT (FOR BANK USE)			
		NAME (Please Print)			
		CHECKS AND OTHER ITEMS ARE RECEIVED FOR DEPOSIT SUBJECT TO THE PROVISIONS OF THE UNIFORM COMMERCIAL CODE OR ANY APPLICABLE COLLECTION AGREEMENT.			
		ACCOUNT NO.			
			TOTAL $		

The only thing on Jennifer's mind was that Christmas was just two days away, and she had no money to buy Andy a present.

Jennifer and Andy were newlyweds, and this was their first Christmas as husband and wife. They had met in college in their junior year. Now Andy was in graduate school full-time, and Jennifer was working as a medical receptionist to support them. When Andy finished his MBA, she would go to graduate school to become a physical therapist. But right now, they could barely make ends meet.

Their studio apartment was scantily furnished with a sofa bed, TV, makeshift bookcases, and table and chairs. Besides Andy's computer, which was a must for school, the only "luxury" items they had were a CD player Andy had gotten for his 21st birthday and a VCR Jennifer's sister had given them as a wedding present.

Andy never studied at home when Jennifer was there because he didn't want her to have to tiptoe around. Besides, she was a big distraction. The young couple hardly saw each other. They never went out, not even to the movies. Jennifer had to settle for occasionally renting videos and watching them alone.

Jennifer knew just what to get Andy. Whenever he was home

he played his old CDs non-stop, and she knew he was dying for some new ones. Jennifer suddenly had an idea. She would sell the VCR. She could probably get $50 or $75 for it at the local video store, which advertised, "We buy used VCRs."

On the day of Christmas eve, Jennifer went to work as usual. Andy spent the day running errands and preparing their Christmas Eve dinner. They had decided to spend Christmas Eve alone, and visit friends and family on Christmas Day. Dinner was perfect. After dessert, they brought out their gifts from their hiding places. Andy opened his first. At the sight of the CDs, his jaw went slack.

"What's the matter?" she asked.

"Nothing," he said. "The CDs are great. It's just that I–uh–sold the CD player to get your gift."

Jennifer turned pale. "Can you get it back?" she asked.

"No," Andy said, "but that doesn't matter. Someday, we'll be able to afford a new one. You open your gift."

Jennifer was still unnerved, but she opened her gift nevertheless. It was a videotape. "I know how much you loved *The Bridges of Madison County*," Andy said. "That's the movie we saw the night I proposed. Now you can watch it anytime you want."

Exercise 1

Find words that mean:

1. to ask someone to get married
2. a temporary substitute
3. a one-room apartment with a kitchen and a bathroom
4. continuously
5. barely
6. to have money for
7. a recently married couple
8. to provide for
9. the third year of college
10. shaken up

Exercise 2

1. "The only thing on Jennifer's mind" means
☐ **A.** there was only one thing that Jennifer minded.
☐ **B.** she was dreaming about only one thing.
☐ **C.** she was thinking about only one thing.

2. "They could barely make ends meet" means
☐ **A.** they couldn't pay their bills.
☐ **B.** they could just pay their bills.
☐ **C.** they never had time to meet.

3. "Andy's computer was a must for school" means
☐ **A.** Andy had to have a computer for his schoolwork.
☐ **B.** Andy's computer was at school.
☐ **C.** Andy's computer was a tool for school.

4. "He didn't want her to have to tiptoe around" means
☐ **A.** he didn't want her to have to dance.
☐ **B.** he didn't want her to have to stay away.
☐ **C.** he didn't want her to have to walk quietly.

5. "She was a big distraction" because
☐ **A.** she made a lot of noise.
☐ **B.** he wanted to spend a lot of time with her instead of studying.
☐ **C.** she watched TV a lot.

6. "Jennifer had to settle for occasionally renting videos" means
☐ **A.** she had to be content with occasionally renting videos.
☐ **B.** she had to go far to occasionally rent videos.
☐ **C.** she had to calm down to occasionally rent videos.

7. "He was dying for some new ones" means
☐ **A.** he was very sick.
☐ **B.** he was willing to kill someone to get new ones.
☐ **C.** he was anxious to get some new ones.

8. "His jaw went slack" means
☐ **A.** his jaw dropped.
☐ **B.** he couldn't move his jaw.
☐ **C.** he pushed out his jaw.

9. "Jennifer turned pale" because
☐ **A.** she was embarrassed.
☐ **B.** she was shocked.
☐ **C.** she was angry.

Unit 16

Language Summary

| make/let | someone | do | something |
| force/allow | | to do | |

Exercise 1

Ben Miller is in prison. He's writing to his mother.
The letter begins:

Write five sentences with *make*, five with *let*, and five with *don't let*.

Parkwood Maximum Security Prison
REGULATIONS, "C" WING

All prisoners must
1. get up at 5 o'clock
2. go to bed at 7:30
3. clean their own cells
4. wear prison uniform at all times
5. work in the prison workshops
6. obey all orders from the guards

Prisoners may
1. have two visitors per month
2. write up to 3 letters a week
3. buy cigarettes and candy from the prison store
4. earn up to $5 a week in the workshops
5. watch TV for 1 hour per day

Prisoners may not
1. have any alcoholic beverages
2. smoke in their cells
3. have radios or cassette players
4. bring money into the prison
5. leave their cells without permission

SIGNED *Harold McVicar* Warden

Exercise 2

Joe was in prison for two months. He has just been released. He's telling a friend about it.

"It was terrible! They forced us to get up at 5 o'clock. They only allowed us two visitors a month, and they didn't allow us to smoke in our cells!"

Write four sentences with *forced*, four with *allowed*, and four with *not allowed*.

Exercise 3

On the day Joe arrived at the prison, he had to go through certain procedures. Write sentences about his experience:

1. (force) They *forced him to* walk into the prison in handcuffs.

2. (make) They .... take off all his clothes.

3. (not allow) They .... keep any of his belongings.

4. (force) They .... take a shower in public.

5. (allow) They eventually .... put on a prisoner's uniform.

6. (not let) They .... keep his hair long.

Unit 17

Language Summary

I'd	like	to do	that.
I'd just	like	that.	

There isn't much choice.

I'd	rather do this./I'd rather not do that.
I'd much	rather do this.
What would you	rather do?

I can't make up my mind.

What do you feel like doing?

Which do you like better?

Which do you prefer, this or that?

I like both.
I don't like any/either of them.

What would you prefer to do, this or that?

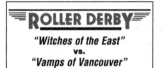

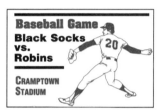

Exercise 1

antique show/circus
Which would you prefer to see, the antique show or the circus?
I'd prefer to see the antique show.

Write questions and answers.

1. ice show/concert
2. air show/art exhibition

Exercise 2

roller derby/wrestling match
Where would you rather go?
I'd rather go to the roller derby.

Write questions and answers.

1. baseball game/tennis match
2. ballet/dog races

Exercise 3

Look at the "Entertainment Guide."
I'd like to see the roller derby.
I wouldn't like to see the wrestling match.

Write ten more sentences.

Exercise 4

Let's go to the wrestling match or dog races tonight.

    I'd rather go to the roller derby.
or *I'd prefer to go to the roller derby.*
or *I'd rather not go to either one.*
or *I'm not much interested in either one. I'd much rather go to
    the baseball game.*

Now answer these questions.

1. Should we go to the air show or the ballet?
2. Do you want to go to the circus or the concert?
3. What are you up for, the tennis match or the dog races?
4. Where would you rather go, the ice show or the
    antique show?
5. I don't really want to go to the baseball game. I'd prefer
    to go to the art exhibition. What about you?

Exercise 5

Look at the Language Summary.

Answer these questions.

1. What color do you like best?
2. Which do you prefer, regular or decaffeinated coffee?
3. Where would you prefer to live, the city or the country?
4. Which would you rather eat, chicken or beef?

Unit 18

Language Summary

They ought to do it./They shouldn't do it.
What should they do?

We	'd	better	do it.
I	had	better not	

Exercise 1

I need some money, and the bank closes in ten minutes.
You ought to go now or *You ought to hurry.*

Continue.

1. We have a long trip, and the gas tank is almost empty.

....

2. She's getting married on Saturday, but she doesn't have a dress.

....

3. His car is in a "no parking" area and a police officer is coming.

....

4. She's just spilled coffee on his new suit.

....

5. It's his parents' anniversary tomorrow.

....

6. There's a fire in the kitchen, and they can't put it out.

....

Exercise 2

Look at these signs. Make sentences about each one.

1. *You'd better not smoke.*

Exercise 3

There is an election for the Middleburg City Council next week. The candidates for the North Middleburg district are Mike Woods and Marjorie Bianco. These are their election platforms.

Vote for MIKE WOODS

1. Spend more money on schools
2. Stop building new highways
3. Make downtown into a pedestrian mall
4. Build more public housing
5. Introduce free buses for senior citizens
6. Increase property taxes

MARJORIE BIANCO
YOUR CANDIDATE FOR CITY COUNCIL

1. Spend more money on the police
2. Build a new freeway
3. Don't make a pedestrian mall (Store owners don't like the plan)
4. Spend less on social services
5. Build an airport near the city
6. Don't increase property taxes

Mike Woods is speaking at a political meeting.

"I think they ought to spend more money on schools. They're spending far too much on highways that we don't need. We shouldn't build new highways."

Make four sentences with *should(n't)* for Mike.

Make six sentences for Marjorie.

Unit 19

Language Summary

try to do	*tell*	*someone to do*
	ask	
keep doing	*help*	

get used to doing

Exercise

Look at these sentences. Put the verbs in parentheses in the correct form.

He enjoys *sitting* in the sun. (sit)
He'd better not *sit* there too long.
He wants *to sit* there all day.

1. Put that cigarette out! You are not allowed .... in here. (smoke)

2. It's hot in here. Would you mind .... the window? (open)

3. He found the questions hard, but he managed .... the examination. (pass)

4. I never read Shakespeare now, because they made me .... it at school. (study)

5. He always travels by train or boat because he's afraid of ....(fly)

6. "Let's go out tonight." "All right. Where do you want .... ?" (go)

7. Your doctor said that you ought .... more exercise. (get)

8. This is a very nice town, but there's nowhere .... at night. (go)

9. When I went to Japan, I couldn't get used to .... on the left. (drive)

10. There's a lot of traffic. We'd better not .... the street here. (cross)

11. I don't know why he resigned. He seemed .... very happy here. (be)

12. I'm tired of .... TV every night. (watch)

13. His doctor advised him .... a specialist. (see)

14. I'll help you. I'm sure you aren't strong enough .... it on your own. (lift)

15. She spends all her time .... comics. (read)

16. My parents were very strict. They wouldn't let me .... out late in the evenings. (stay)

17. A kettle is used for .... water. (boil)

18. She's working too hard. She's too tired .... anything when she gets home. (do)

19. The robbers forced the manager .... the safe. (open)

20. I hope .... my sister in Los Angeles next year. (visit)

21. She's not interested in .... money; her father's a millionaire. (earn)

22. Don't give up yet; we have to keep .... (try)

23. I'd rather .... happy than rich. (be)

24. She went to the police because her neighbor tried .... her. (rob)

25. I was very happy .... your news. (hear)

26. Take your time. I don't mind .... (wait)

27. I'd rather not .... about that. (talk)

28. We're going to the beach tomorrow. Would you like .... with us? (come)

29. She won't be long. She just has two more phone calls .... (make)

30. He didn't want to go to work, so he pretended .... sick. (be)

31. I gave up .... five years ago. (smoke)

32. I'm bored with .... the same clothes every day. (wear)

33. The book was very hard .... (understand)

34. Neither of them could find a job, so they both decided .... to Houston. (move)

35. She's very confident. She expects .... the election. (win)

36. I'm not here .... my time! (waste)

37. They won't let you .... the United States without a visa. (enter)

38. He joined the navy .... the world. (see)

39. I wonder if you'd be kind enough .... me? (help)

40. Jim Carrey's movies always make me .... (laugh)

Unit 20

Language Summary

It's certainly I'm (almost) certain …	It must be …	It's possible but a little less possible than *may*.	It might be …
It's probably …	It could be … It may be …	It's probably not …	It can't be …
		It's definitely not …	It couldn't be …

Exercise 1

What's that in the sky? Is it from outer space?
(impossible) *It can't be from outer space.*

Continue.

1. Is this table Victorian?

   (probably) ....

2. Who's that? I think it's Michael Jackson!

   (possibly, but a little less possible than may) ....

   ....

3. She has a private plane. Is she very rich? (almost certain)

   ....

4. That man says he's 130 years old.

   (almost impossible) ....

   ....

Exercise 2

A spy has "bugged" this hotel room. (He's hidden a small microphone somewhere.) Where do you think it is?
It could be under the bed.
It might even be under the pillow.

Write sentences with *could, may,* and *might*.

1. ....

2. ....

3. ....

4. ....

5. ....

6. ....

7. ....

8. ....

Exercise 3

Mr. Roger J. Smith
What do you think the initial stands for?
It could be John. It could be James. It could be Joseph. It might be Julius!

Continue.

1. Ms. Sally M. Grooms ....

   ....

2. Mr. Michael R. Wilson ....

   ....

3. Mrs. Dolores F. Parker...

   ....

continued

4. Miss B. Ellen Matthews ....

....

5. Mr. W. Craig Phillips ....

....

Exercise 4

The police are looking for a murderer. They know it was a thin, white man in his 30s, of average height with short hair, a mustache, and glasses. These are the six suspects in a police lineup.

It couldn't be Chapman, because he doesn't have a mustache.

Write four sentences with *couldn't* and one with *must*.

1. ....

2. ....

3. ....

4. ....

5. ....

Exercise 5

My grandmother can remember the first car in our town. *She must be very old.*

Continue.

1. My sister won the lottery three times last year. ....

....

2. My father has a Cadillac and a Corvette. ....

....

3. My brother is only 15, but he's going to college next year.

....

4. My uncle can lift 440 pounds (200 kg). ....

....

5. My mother volunteers at a hospital twice a week. ....

....

6. My cousin takes five showers a day. ....

....

7. My grandfather runs ten marathons a year. ....

....

8. My aunt is a professional model. ....

....

9. Our dog bites everyone who comes to our house. ....

....

10. My father-in-law is a violinist with the Philharmonic

Orchestra. ....

....

11. My nephew weighed 13 pounds (6 kg) when he was

born. ....

....

12. My nieces are both champion gymnasts. ....

....

13. Our house has five bedrooms. ....

....

14. My paintings have been exhibited in a gallery. ....

....

15. Three cars have had accidents on that corner this year.

....

....

16. My brother-in-law plays professional basketball. ....

....

....

Unit 21

Language Summary

They	must may might can't could couldn't	be having a party.

She's	probably possibly	having a party.
to have	a fight a good time a party	

Exercise 1

Katherine is sitting in the theater.
She must be watching a movie/She's probably watching a movie.
What do you think these people are doing?

1. James is sitting in a restaurant.

....

2. Sheila is walking through an art gallery.

....

3. Gail and Tomasina are standing in a video store.

....

4. Lynn is in her car on the freeway in California.

....

5. José and Victoria are sitting in the library.

....

6. Richard is sitting in a football stadium.

....

Exercise 2

Look! He's sawing that woman in half!
He couldn't be sawing her in half. It must be a trick.

Continue.

1. Look! He's eating fire! ....

....

....

2. Look! He's floating in midair! ....

....

....

3. Look! He's making that woman disappear! ....

....

....

4. Look! That dog is talking to him! ....

....

....

5. Look! He's taking money from his ear! ....

....

....

6. Look! He's pulling rabbits from his hat! ....

....

....

7. Look! He's taking birds out of his mouth! ....

....

....

8. Look! He's swallowing a sword! ....

....

....

continued

Exercise 3

	Los Angeles San Francisco	Chicago Mexico City	Venezuela Bolivia Chile	Greenland		Most of Europe Zaire	Moscow Iraq	Pakistan	Malaysia		Japan		New Zealand

International Date Line	AM	NOON	PM	AM

1:00	2:00	3:00	4:00	5:00	6:00	7:00	8:00	9:00	10:00	11:00	12:00	13:00	14:00	15:00	16:00	17:00	18:00	19:00	20:00	21:00	22:00	23:00	24:00

Alaska	Denver	Montreal New York Colombia Peru	Eastern Brazil Argentina	England Algeria	Greece Turkey Egypt	Arabian Gulf	India	China	Eastern Australia

Alaska is four hours behind Mexico.
China is eight hours ahead of England.

Write four more sentences.

1. ....

2. ....

3. ....

4. ....

Exercise 4

Write four sentences using ... *behind my country/city* and *ahead of my country/city.*

1. ....

2. ....

3. ....

4. ....

Exercise 5

What time is it here, right now? ....

Look at this example.

I live in New York. I'm writing this at 10:00 PM.
What do you think someone is doing in Italy?
It's 4 AM there now.   *They must be sleeping./They're probably sleeping.*

What do you think someone is doing in California?
It's 7:00 PM there now.   *They're probably not working./ They may be having dinner./ They might be talking to some friends./They might be watching television.*

Choose six places and write sentences about what people might be doing now.

Italy.   *It's (time) there now. They must be sleeping. They're probably sleeping.*

1. ....

2. ....

3. ....

4. ....

5. ....

6. ....

Unit 22

Language Summary

| They | should (not)/are (not) supposed to | be doing that. |
| | had better (not)/would rather (not) | |

Exercise 1

Rafael Cordero is a business executive. He's very overweight, and he's just checked into a health spa. It's his first day.

A. *He's drinking beet juice.*

B. *He'd rather not be drinking beet juice.*

C. *He'd rather be drinking champagne.*

A. ....

B. ....

C. ....

A. ....

B. ....

C. ....

A. ....

B. ....

C. ....

Exercise 2

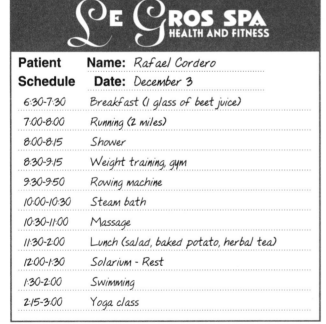

LE GROS SPA
HEALTH AND FITNESS

Patient	**Name:** Rafael Cordero
Schedule	**Date:** December 3
6:30-7:30	Breakfast (1 glass of beet juice)
7:00-8:00	Running (2 miles)
8:00-8:15	Shower
8:30-9:15	Weight training, gym
9:30-9:50	Rowing machine
10:00-10:30	Steam bath
10:30-11:00	Massage
11:30-2:00	Lunch (salad, baked potato, herbal tea)
12:00-1:30	Solarium - Rest
1:30-2:00	Swimming
2:15-3:00	Yoga class

It's the second day. Mr. Cordero has disappeared from the spa. They haven't been able to find him all morning. At 6:45 the Director said, *"Where's Mr. Cordero? He's supposed to be having breakfast!"*

What did he say at the following times?

7:30 ....

8:10 ....

8:45 ....

9:40 ....

10:15 ....

11:00 ....

11:45 ....

12:45 ....

1:45 ....

2:45 ....

continued

Look at Exercise 2. Make sentences with *He should be doing ...* and *He ought to be doing ....*

1. ....
2. ....
3. ....
4. ....
5. ....

6. ....
7. ....
8. ....
9. ....
10. ....

At 3:00 the Director got a phone call from a nearby restaurant. They asked him to come and pick up Mr. Cordero. When he got there, this is what he said:
Mr. Cordero! You aren't supposed to be sitting in a restaurant.

Write three more sentences.

1. ....
2. ....
3. ....

Look at Exercise 4.

Make four sentences with *You shouldn't be doing ...*

1. ....
2. ....

3. ....
4. ....

The Director said, "This isn't good enough, Mr. Cordero. Le Gros Spa is very expensive. If you want to stay, you'll have to follow our program. If not, you'll have to leave and we won't be able to refund your money. So tomorrow at 6:45 you'd better be having breakfast!"

Look at the schedule in Exercise 2, and write ten sentences with *You'd better ...* and four sentences with *You'd better not ....*

1. ....
2. ....
3. ....
4. ....
5. ....
6. ....
7. ....

8. ....
9. ....
10. ....
11. ....
12. ....
13. ....
14. ....

The hospital was small and private with just one entrance. Michael looked through the window down into the street. There was a curved courtyard that had steps leading down into the street and the street was empty of cars. But whoever came into the hospital would have to come through that entrance. He knew he didn't have much time so he ran out of the room and down the four flights and through the wide doors of the ground floor entrance. Off to the side he saw the ambulance yard and there was no car there, no ambulances either.

Michael stood on the sidewalk outside the hospital and lit a cigarette. He unbuttoned his coat and stood in the light of a lamppost so that his features could be seen. A young man was walking swiftly down from Ninth Avenue, a package under his arm. His face was familiar when he came under the lamplight but Michael could not place it. But the young man stopped in front of him and put out his hand, saying in a heavy Italian accent, "Don Michael, do you remember me? Enzo, the baker's helper to Nazorine the Paniterra; his son-in-law. Your father saved my life by getting the government to let me stay in America."

Michael shook his hand. He remembered him now.

Enzo went on, "I've come to pay my respects to your father. Will they let me into the hospital so late?"

Michael smiled and shook his head. "No, but thanks anyway. I'll tell the Don you came." A car came roaring down the street and Michael was instantly alert. He said to Enzo, "Leave here quickly. There may be trouble. You don't want to get involved with the police."

He saw the look of fear on the young Italian's face. Trouble with the police might mean being deported or refusal of citizenship. But the young man stood fast. He whispered in Italian, "If there's trouble I'll stay to help. I owe it to the Godfather."

Michael was touched. He was about to tell the young man to go away again, but then he thought, why not let him stay? Two men in front of the hospital might scare off any of Sollozzo's crew sent to do a job. One man almost certainly would not. They both stood under the lamppost in the cold December night.

...g on glass... ...any bri... accent. He lures Sugar to Fielding's yacht, which he pretends is his. Junior is

From *The Godfather* by Mario Puzo. G.P. Putnam's Sons, New York, 1969.

Exercise 1

Find words that mean:

1. set on fire
2. generally known
3. making a loud, deep sound
4. the parts of a face
5. a style of speech or pronunciation
6. thick
7. at once
8. not public
9. an open space surrounded by walls
10. to frighten someone away
11. series of stairs
12. watchful
13. to be made to leave a country
14. quickly

Exercise 2

1. "The young man had a heavy shock of black hair" means
   - ☐ **A.** he had a long, black beard.
   - ☐ **B.** he had a bushy quantity of black hair.
   - ☐ **C.** his black hair was standing straight up.

2. "His face was familiar when he came under the lamplight but Michael could not place it" means
   - ☐ **A.** Michael thought he knew him, but he couldn't remember where he knew him from.
   - ☐ **B.** Michael thought he knew him, but he couldn't see his face clearly.
   - ☐ **C.** Michael thought he knew him, but he couldn't find him.

3. "I've come to pay my respects to your father" means
   - ☐ **A.** he's come to give Michael's father the money he owes him.
   - ☐ **B.** he's come to show Michael's father that he thinks highly of him.
   - ☐ **C.** he's come to bribe Michael's father.

4. "The young man stood fast" means
   - ☐ **A.** he didn't move.
   - ☐ **B.** he ran away quickly.
   - ☐ **C.** he got up fast.

5. "Michael was touched" means
   - ☐ **A.** he was contacted.
   - ☐ **B.** he was tapped.
   - ☐ **C.** he was moved emotionally.

Exercise 3

Answer these questions.

1. Who is in the hospital?
   - ☐ **A.** Michael's father
   - ☐ **B.** Enzo's father-in-law
   - ☐ **C.** the police

2. Who is Michael's father?
   - ☐ **A.** a baker's helper
   - ☐ **B.** the Godfather
   - ☐ **C.** a government worker

3. Who do you think Sollozzo is?
   - ☐ **A.** an enemy of the Godfather's
   - ☐ **B.** a relative of Enzo's
   - ☐ **C.** a friend of Michael's

4. Why didn't Michael tell Enzo to go away?
   - ☐ **A.** because he was enjoying talking to him
   - ☐ **B.** because Enzo had come to see the Godfather
   - ☐ **C.** because Enzo could help Michael protect the Godfather

5. What would Sollozzo's crew be coming to do?
   - ☐ **A.** to work at the hospital
   - ☐ **B.** to harm the Godfather or his family
   - ☐ **C.** to meet the police

Unit 24

Exercise 1

"I still can't believe it happened. I drive a BMW convertible, and it was a scorching hot day so the top was down. I had taken off my jacket and put it on the passenger seat. Anyway, I was driving along Edgemont Street and I stopped at a traffic light. I was sitting there, listening to the radio and waiting for the light to change. Suddenly a young man reached over the side of the car, grabbed my jacket, and disappeared into the crowd. The light turned green and all the cars behind me began blowing their horns. I just didn't know what to do! My wallet was in the inside jacket pocket, so was my checkbook…and my credit cards."

Answer these questions.

1. What kind of car does he drive? ....

2. What was the weather like? ....

3. What had he done? ....

4. Where had he put his jacket? ....

5. Where was he driving? ....

6. Where did he stop? ....

7. What was he doing? ....

8. What did the young man do? ....

9. What did the other cars begin doing? ....

10. What was in his jacket pocket? ....

Exercise 2

He stopped by a public phone and called the police. A police officer arrived, and he told the police officer what had happened. The police officer wrote it all down and then checked through the statement.
The top was down, *wasn't it?*

Fill in the tag questions.

1. You'd taken your jacket off, ...

2. You'd put it on the passenger seat, ...

3. You were driving along Edgemont Street, ...

4. You stopped at the traffic light, ...

5. You were listening to the radio, ...

6. You weren't looking at the street, ...

7. He grabbed your jacket, ...

8. You didn't see his face, ...

9. He ran into the crowd, ...

10. The other cars began blowing their horns, ...

Exercise 3

It's a nice day, *isn't it?* It isn't going to rain, *is it?*

1. You aren't hungry, ...

2. He doesn't smoke, ...

3. You drive a Porsche, ...

4. She hasn't gotten there yet, ...

5. You'd rather play tennis, ...

6. We'll see her later, ...

7. There weren't enough tickets, ...

8. He couldn't copy it, ...

9. You've got enough cash, ...

10. There was a lot to do, ...

11. You won't tell anybody, ...

12. I'm not late, ...

13. They all speak English, ...

14. You're supposed to be helping, ...

15. You shouldn't be out of bed, ...

16. They'd prefer to stay home, ...

17. She won last year, too, ...

18. I can see him now, ...

Unit 25

Language Summary

Could	it	have been	him? her? them?

It	must could may (not) might (not) couldn't	have been	him. her. them.

Could	he she they	have	done it? killed him? shot him?

He She They	must could may (not) might (not) couldn't	have	done it. killed him. shot him.

Exercise

Five years ago, Betty Wallace was very poor. Now she's a millionaire.

She must have been very lucky.
She might have married a rich man.
She may have been successful in business.
She could have robbed a bank.
or something else.

Make two sentences about each of these situations.

1. The door was locked, but the thief managed to get into the hotel room.

....

....

2. Mr. and Mrs. Sullivan are very worried. Their son, Hal, usually gets home from school at 4:30. It's 6:00 and he hasn't arrived yet.

....

....

3. Maureen phoned her boss at 9:00 and said she was too sick to come to work. At 9:30 her boss called Maureen's house, and there was no answer.

....

....

4. Penny made a date with Gregg. They planned to meet outside the theater at 7:30. It's 8:00 and he hasn't shown up.

....

....

5. Vicky Lester escaped from prison. The police checked all the airports, train stations, bus depots, and ports, but they weren't able to find her.

....

....

6. Jake Rowley robbed a bank, stole a plane, and parachuted out over the Amazon jungle. He's never been seen since.

....

....

7. The T.C. Cannon painting "Apache Chief," which was stolen two years ago, is still missing. It is so famous that it is impossible to sell.

....

....

8. A month ago, Jack was 20 pounds underweight. Now he's just right

....

....

9. Five years ago, Fran Wright was a millionaire. Now she's penniless.

....

....

10. A man has just wandered into the Portstown police station. He has no documents or identification but is wearing good clothes. He's lost his memory.

....

....

11. Terry Singleton was shipwrecked and survived on a desert island alone for two years before she was rescued.

....

....

12. Dave Armfield was on television last night. He said he was born in 1880.

....

....

13. At 5:00 in the morning, on an empty highway, a car ran into a bridge at 100 mph. The driver was killed.

....

....

14. Paul has just read a letter, and he's crying.

....

....

15. Wendy can't stop laughing.

....

....

Look at this letter:

Mr. William Hynes
1130 Fifth Avenue
Chula Vista, CA 92011

Customer Relations
Mistral Foods, Inc.
31900 Ninth Avenue
Laguna Niguel, CA 92677

1130 Fifth Avenue
Chula Vista, CA 92011

March 8, 1996

Customer Relations
Mistral Foods, Inc.
31900 Ninth Avenue
Laguna Niguel, CA 92677

Dear Sir or Madam:

I bought a can of your "Baked Beans in Tomato Sauce" at a FoodSmart in Chula Vista a few days ago. The lot number is A0305742.

When I put the beans into a saucepan to heat them, I noticed a piece of glass, which I have saved. I was very upset. I could have cut my mouth, or broken a tooth, or worse. I might even have given it to my three-year-old son, and he might have swallowed it!

I hope to hear from you soon.

Sincerely yours,

William Hynes

William Hynes

Exercise 1

Sandy Cooper lives at 222 Greenwood Avenue in La Jolla, California. Her zip code is 92037. She had just bought a used car. It was a Calypso, license plate number CRA 749. It had a one-year warranty. Just after she left the used-car lot, the brakes failed on a steep hill. She couldn't stop and just missed a group of children waiting for a school bus. She then hit a police car. Fortunately, no one was hurt.

Write a letter to the used-car dealer. Say what happened and what might have happened.

Exercise 2

Look at these notes.

Lorraine Campbell, 432 Doyle Drive, St. Joseph, Missouri, 64503. Gas service man/install new gas stove. She/go to work. Told service man/let himself out when/finished. Came back/6 o'clock. House/full of gas. She/heavy smoker. Luckily/not smoking.

Write a letter to the Consumer Protection Agency. Say what happened and what might have happened.

Exercise 3

Look at these notes.

Henry Wade, 83 years old. 1621 Cherokee Road, Tulsa, Oklahoma, 74102. Standing in line/last bus. Last in line. Bus came. Driver/everybody/hurry. He/getting on/bus/pulled away. Almost fell off. Fortunately/let go of bar. Not hurt. Had to take/taxi home.

Write to the Tulsa Bus Company. Explain what happened. Say what might have happened.

Exercise 4

Have you ever found anything in a can or box of food? Have you ever had an accident? nearly had an accident? hurt yourself because of someone else's negligence?

Write a letter saying what happened and what might have happened.

Unit 27

Language Summary

He	should shouldn't ought not to	have done that.

Exercise 1

Anthony and Laura Diamond took a trip to the Mediterranean arranged by Sunshine Tours. It was disastrous. When they got back, Laura went to see the travel agent.
The plane didn't take off on time.
It should have taken off on time.

What else should have happened? Write your answers.

1. They didn't give us a meal on the plane.

2. The representative didn't meet us at the airport.
3. You hadn't sent the reservation to the hotel.
4. There were no rooms for us at the hotel.
5. They didn't find us another hotel.
6. They didn't apologize.

Exercise 2

Joyce Leibling's driver's license was suspended last month. In court, the police read out all the things she had done.
She backed up on a main highway.
She shouldn't have backed up on a main highway.

What else shouldn't she have done? Write your answers.

1. She forgot to signal that she was turning.
2. She drove too fast.
3. She went through a red light.
4. She had her arm around her boyfriend.
5. She hit a lamppost.
6. She made an illegal U-turn.

Exercise 3

Priscilla Raleigh misbehaved in school. The principal has just called Mrs. Raleigh to tell her about Priscilla's behavior.
She didn't pay attention to her teacher.
She ought to have paid attention to her teacher.
She chewed gum in gym class.
She shouldn't have chewed gum in gym class.

What other things did he say? Write your answers.

1. She wrote bad words on the chalkboard.
2. She didn't do her homework.
3. She took another child's book.
4. She threw an eraser at another child.
5. She didn't bring a pen to school.
6. She rode her bicycle in the halls.
7. She refused to play her instrument in music class.
8. She didn't come to see me yesterday.
9. She was late every day last week.
10. She brought a dog into a classroom.

Exercise 4

Look at this letter of complaint, and write an answer from the company.

2255 University Hills
Toledo, Ohio 43606
August 27, 1996

Customer Service
Alexandoff Department Store
420 Main Street
Toledo, Ohio 43601

Dear Sir or Madam:
    I bought a hair dryer at your store in the University Plaza Mall last week. I'm afraid I didn't keep the receipt, and I threw away the box and the guarantee.
    When I opened the box, I found it was the wrong color. I had asked for beige, and it was black. I didn't take it back to the store then because I was too busy. The first time I used it, I turned it on and it seemed to be working fine. But when I put it down on the counter, it started to get very hot, and I could smell something burning. Then the dryer clicked off and wouldn't go on again. It has not worked since, and the dryer is completely useless.
    I went back to the store with the dryer and spoke to the branch manager. He refused to exchange it and was very rude. Please refund my $26.80.

Sincerely yours,

Sandra Douglas

Sandra Douglas

Unit 28 (Review)

Language Summary

Someone did it ... it was done.
Someone did them ... they were done.

Someone had done it ... it had been done.

Someone was doing it ... it was being done.
Someone was doing them ... they were being done.

Exercise 1

Complete this table.

-an/-ian/-nian		-ish		-ese	
Colombia	*Colombian*	Denmark	*Danish*	Sudan	*Sudanese*
Argentina	....	Finland	....	Senegal	....
Austria	....	Ireland	....	Portugal	....
Belgium	....	Poland	....	Japan	....
Brazil	....	Sweden	....	Burma	....
Canada	....	Turkey	...:.............................	China	....
Egypt	....	Britain	....	Lebanon	....
Venezuela	....	England	....	Malta	....
Germany	....	Scotland	....	Nepal	....
Panama	....	Spain	....	Vietnam	....
Mexico	....				
Russia	....				
United States	....				

-i		others			
Pakistan	*Pakistani*	Czech Republic	*Czech*	The Netherlands	....
Iraq	....	France	....	Switzerland	....
Kuwait	....	Greece	....	Thailand	....
		Iceland	....	Wales	....

Exercise 2

"Someone gave me a present."
You can say　**A.** *"I was given a present."*
　　　　　　　B. *"A present was given to me."*
"I was given a present" is more usual.

Change these sentences in both ways.

1. The boss promised them a raise.
2. The company had offered her a good job.
3. His father had left him a fortune.
4. They sent me a telegram.
5. Someone had given them a map of the area.
6. Someone showed her the new house.

Exercise 3

Dorothy Booker was born in a small town in Texas. She moved away when she was a child. The town has had an economic "boom" and when she returned recently, everything had changed. The whole area looked like a building site! They were building new houses.
New houses were being built.

Continue.

1. They were constructing a new shopping mall.
2. They were planting trees everywhere.
3. They were constructing roads.
4. They were building a school.
5. They were demolishing old houses.

Exercise 4

Rudy was played by Joe Revolta.

Write 12 more sentences.

SLASH!
New Rock Musical
★ *Producer* **BOB STALEWOOD**
★ *Director* **CHARLES ORSON**
★ *Screenplay* **MARY JO ALLEN**

From an original story by **TRUMAN HOOD**
Music composed by **HAZEL WILCOX**
Performed by **THE FUZZ**
TITLE SONG "SLASH" sung by **BETH LANG**
Dance sequences choreographed by **Sheila Darwin**
Fight sequences coached by **Jerry Floyd**

FEATURING　**JOE REVOLTA** as Rudy
　　　　　　CYNTHIA NEWTON as Carmen
　　　Also starring　**WILLIAM PAINE** as the Priest
　　　　　　　and **RITA COLON** as Big Mama

A TAC FILM TRANS AMERICA CORP

Unit 29

Language Summary

| They | must
could
may
might
might even
couldn't
can't
should
shouldn't | have been doing it. |

He jumped in to save the others.
They launched a boat to rescue them

Exercise 1

1. *He must have been drinking.*

2. ....

3. ....

4. ....

5. ....

6. ....

Exercise 2

What do you think these people were doing a short time ago? Write sentences with: *may/might/could have been doing.*

1. A. ....

   B. ....

   C. ....

2. A. ....

   B. ....

   C. ....

3. A. ....

   B. ....

   C. ....

continued

Exercise 3

Someone says, "I heard Maria speaking Chinese." You know she doesn't speak Chinese.
She couldn't have been speaking Chinese.

1. The traffic officer says, "You were doing 90 mph." You know the maximum speed of your car is 80 mph.

....

....

2. Someone says, "I saw Jane sitting in a coffee shop." You know she is out of town.

....

....

3. Someone says, "I saw Jack eating in the Steak House." You know he's a vegetarian.

....

....

4. Someone says, "Our baby was reading Shakespeare!"

....

....

Exercise 4

She was smoking near the gas pump.
She shouldn't have been smoking near the gas pump.

1. The night guard was sleeping on duty. ....

....

2. He was laughing during the funeral. ....

....

3. She was driving at 60 mph through downtown. ....

....

4. They were eating in the library. ....

....

Exercise 5

He was driving on the right in England when he crashed.

A. *He shouldn't have been driving on the right.*
B. *He should have been driving on the left.*

1. The student was sleeping during class.

A. ....

B. ....

2. The basketball player was arguing with the referee when the other team scored.

A. ....

B. ....

3. He was watching TV when the milk boiled over.

A. ....

B. ....

4. She was looking at an attractive man when she walked into the lamppost.

A. ....

B. ....

Exercise 6

They called for help, so she ran in. *She ran in to help them.*

1. He wanted to see her, so he took the train.

....

2. They tried to get into the office, but they didn't have a pass.

....

3. I had to meet my mother at the theater, so I left work early.

....

4. We couldn't pay for the CD because we didn't have enough money.

....

Now Playing at the Pearl Street Cinema

A MARILYN MONROE FILM RETROSPECTIVE

SUNDAY
Some Like It Hot ('59)

MONDAY
Gentlemen Prefer Blondes ('53)

TUESDAY
The Misfits ('61)

WEDNESDAY
How to Marry a Millionaire ('53)

THURSDAY
Niagara ('52)

FRIDAY
The Seven Year Itch ('55)

SATURDAY
Let's Make Love ('60)

SOME LIKE IT HOT

Released: 1959
Producer: Billy Wilder for the Mirisch Company; released by United Artists
Director: Billy Wilder
Screenplay: Billy Wilder and I.A.L. Diamond; suggested by a story by R. Theoren and M. Logan
Cinematographer: Charles Lang
Editor: Arthur Schmidt
Costume Designer: Orry-Kelly
Principal Characters:

Sugar	Marilyn Monroe
Joe/Josephine/Junior	Tony Curtis
Jerry/Daphne	Jack Lemmon
Spats Colombo	George Raft
Mulligan	Pat O'Brien
Osgood Fielding III	Joe E. Brown

Some Like It Hot is a wild, madcap comedy set in the 1920s. The story begins when two musicians, Joe and Jerry, accidentally witness the St. Valentine's Day massacre–the murder of seven Chicago gangsters by a rival mob. Fleeing Spats Colombo and his gang, who are hot on their trail, Joe and Jerry come across an all-female touring band. They disguise themselves as women–Joe as Josephine and Jerry as Daphne–and join the band.

One of the other band members is Sugar, a lonely and beautiful ukelele-strumming singer with a bit of a drinking problem. Sugar, of course, thinks Joe is Josephine and becomes one of her best "girl friends," confiding in her the kind of man she is looking for. In the meantime, Joe has fallen in love with Sugar. Joe convinces Jerry, as Daphne, to encourage the advances of Osgood Fielding III, a wealthy ladies' man. Daphne flirts with Fielding and keeps him distracted, which gives Joe the opportunity to take the identity of a "Junior," putting on glasses and affecting a phony British accent. He lures Sugar to Fielding's yacht, which he pretends is his. Junior is a rich young man with a problem–he gets no thrill from women–and Sugar wants to help him overcome it.

Meanwhile, Daphne has been spending time with Fielding, including a night of dancing the tango. The silliness of the tangled identities reaches a peak when Daphne agrees to marry Fielding. "It's my only chance to marry a millionaire," says Jerry.

Suddenly the mob appears, and Joe and Jerry think their number is up. Instead, the mobsters kill each other off, with Spats being killed by an assassin who pops out of a birthday cake.

Joe is now ready to tell the unsuspecting Sugar the truth about Junior and Jerry realizes he has to tell Fielding that he is Daphne. At the end of the movie, Jerry tears off his wig, revealing his true identity. Fielding, apparently unfazed by the revelation, simply replies, "Well, nobody's perfect."

Exercise 1

Find words that mean:

1. trusting
2. excitement
3. sidetracked
4. telling one's most private thoughts
5. killing of a lot of people
6. kids around with in a sexual way
7. draws
8. faking
9. crazy
10. change their appearance
11. beat
12. rips off
13. competing
14. making known
15. not affected
16. mixed up

Exercise 2

1. "hot on their trail" means
   - ☐ **A.** very angry
   - ☐ **B.** currently popular
   - ☐ **C.** following close behind

2. "come across" means
   - ☐ **A.** please
   - ☐ **B.** arrive at the same time as
   - ☐ **C.** meet by chance

3. "a drinking problem" means
   - ☐ **A.** a problem swallowing
   - ☐ **B.** a problem of habitually drinking too much alcohol
   - ☐ **C.** a problem of not drinking enough water

4. "encourage the advances" means
   - ☐ **A.** encourage the attempts to get to know each other
   - ☐ **B.** encourage the promotion
   - ☐ **C.** encourage the improvement

5. "a lady's man" means
   - ☐ **A.** a man who likes to wear women's clothes
   - ☐ **B.** a man who likes the company of women
   - ☐ **C.** a man who is faithful to his wife

6. "reaches a peak" means
   - ☐ **A.** reaches a maximum
   - ☐ **B.** reaches the top of a mountain
   - ☐ **C.** reaches an agreement

7. "their number is up" means
   - ☐ **A.** they have a winning lottery ticket
   - ☐ **B.** they are on the point of death
   - ☐ **C.** they have to leave

Unit 31

Language Summary

Sorry.
I'm (terribly) sorry.
I really am very sorry.
I'm so sorry.
I just want(ed) to apologize.

I didn't mean to do that.
I didn't realize I had to do that.
It was so dumb of me to do that.
It won't happen again.
It wasn't my fault.
What more can I say?

Don't worry about it.
It really doesn't matter.
Forget it.
It's all right.
It's no big deal.
I don't want to hear another word about it.

Exercise

Look at these sentences. Put the numbers in the appropriate blanks below. Read all of the sentences carefully before you begin.

1. I'm very sorry, officer. I just didn't see the red light.
2. Yes, you're right. It was very careless of me. I'm sorry. I hope you're not hurt.
3. I must have dialed the wrong number. Sorry.
4. It is? Oh, yes. I'm really sorry. It looks just like mine.
5. Oh, my goodness! It is? I didn't realize it. I thought it was the men's room. Sorry.
6. I'm sorry. I didn't notice. Where's the end?
7. Oh really? I didn't know it was a private club. I'm sorry.
8. I'm terribly sorry. I thought you were someone else.
9. Yes, I know. I'm sorry, but I lost your number.
10. Of course it is. How dumb of me! I don't usually forget names.
11. I'm very sorry. I didn't realize it was reserved.
12. No, not this time. The alarm clock didn't go off. I'm sorry I'm late again. It won't happen again.
13. I really must apologize. I thought I had my wallet with me.
14. I'm sorry. I didn't mean to ignore you. I just didn't see you, that's all.

Hey! That's my coat! 4 . . . .

A. Ouch! That's my foot. . . . .

B. You can't come in here. Members only. . . . .

C. Who? I've never heard of him. . . . .

D. You promised to call me. . . . .

E. Smith. Helen Smith. . . . .

F. Why didn't you say hello to me yesterday? . . . .

G. You didn't miss the bus again, did you? . . . .

H. There's a line, you know. . . . .

I. Can I see your driver's license, sir? . . . .

J. I'm afraid you're sitting in my seat. . . . .

K. This is the ladies' room! . . . .

L. Who are you? I've never met you before in my life. . . . .

M. You can pay me next time. You are a regular customer. . . . .

Unit 32

Language Summary

Stop Remember	doing

Stop Remember Forget	to do

Exercise 1

Butcher's
Bank ✓
Bakery
Grocery store ✓
Post office ✓
Dry Cleaner's
Drugstore ✓
Newsstand
Florist ✓
Toy store ✓

Linda is on a business trip. Her husband, Chris, is taking care of the children. Linda gave him a shopping list. He didn't remember to get everything, but he did get some of the things.
He forgot to get some meat.
He remembered to get some money.

Write eight more sentences.

1. ....

2. ....

3. ....

4. ....

5. ....

6. ....

7. ....

8. ....

Exercise 2

He stopped at the bank to get some money.

Write five more sentences.

1. ....

2. ....

3. ....

4. ....

5. ....

Exercise 3

Ten years ago Patricia was a rich young woman. She used to drink, smoke, gamble, eat in expensive restaurants, and go out with wild men. Eight years ago everything changed. She joined a religious order and became a nun. Her name is now Sister Margaret Anne.
She stopped drinking eight years ago.

Write four more sentences.

1. ....

2. ....

3. ....

4. ....

Exercise 4

What can you remember doing in elementary school?
I can remember listening to stories.
I remember learning to read.

Write four more sentences.

1. ....

2. ....

3. ....

4. ....

continued

She was writing. The telephone rang, and she answered it.

A. *She stopped writing.*

B. *She stopped to answer the phone.*

1. The girls were playing basketball. A Concorde flew over. Everybody looked up in the air.

A. ....

B. ....

2. She was driving along the highway. She felt tired. She had a cup of coffee.

A. ....

B. ....

3. During the volleyball game someone brought some lemonade onto the field for the players.

A. ....

B. ....

4. The teacher gave the students a five-minute break.

A. ....

B. ....

5. In the middle of the concert, the guitarist had to change a string.

A. ....

B. ....

6. During the speech the candidate had to blow her nose.

A. ....

B. ....

WATCH OUT!
There's a thief in the area.

When you are leaving your house to go on vacation, remember to

1. lock all the doors
2. close all the windows
3. turn off all the lights
4. shut all the curtains
5. lock away any ladders or tools in the garage

In addition, make arrangements to have your mail and newspaper subscriptions held. Ask your neighbors to check your house every day.

WINFIELD POLICE

Kathleen Nolan is a very careful woman. When she went on vacation recently, she remembered all the precautions.
She remembered to lock all the doors.

Write four more sentences.

1. ....

....

2. ....

....

3. ....

....

4. ....

....

When she got back from her vacation, she was very worried because the living room curtains were open, the bedroom window was open, and her ladder was leaning against the wall. The front door was also open, and the lights were on in the hall.
She was worried because she remembered shutting the curtains.

Write four more sentences.

1. ....

2. ....

3. ....

4. ....

Walter Elias Disney

Walt Disney was born on December 5, 1901, in Chicago. His father was Irish-Canadian, and his mother was German-American. Disney attended McKinley High School in Chicago, and left at the age of 17 to become an ambulance driver in World War I. In 1919 he moved to Kansas City and became a commercial artist. He went to Hollywood in 1923 to become an animator, working on cartoon films. He was married in 1925 to Lillian Bounds. He drew the first Mickey Mouse cartoon in 1928. He was the first producer to use Technicolor, on *Flowers and Trees* in 1933. By 1934 he employed a staff of 700. He created Donald Duck in 1934.

In 1937 he made the first full-length animated movie, *Snow White and the Seven Dwarfs*. Over the next thirty years he made a series of successful animated movies, including *Pinocchio* (1939), *Fantasia* (1940), *Bambi* (1943), *The Lady and the Tramp* (1956), *101 Dalmations* (1956), and the posthumous *The Jungle* Book (1967). His series of "True Life Adventures," which were animal documentaries, were also very popular. His studio also made regular feature-length movies for children, such as *20,000 Leagues Under the Sea*. In 1955 Disneyland was opened in California, and this was followed in 1971 by Disney World in Florida. Disney died on December 15, 1966, in Burbank, California, at the age of 65. His movies are still shown regularly at theaters and on TV and, because of their timeless quality, will continue to be shown for years to come.

Look at these notes on Disney.

WALTER ELIAS DISNEY 12/5/01–12/15/66. Born Chicago. Father: Irish-Canadian. Mother: German-American. McKinley High Sch., Chi. to 17. Then ambulance driver in WW 1. 1919—Kansas City: Commercial artist. 1923—Hollywood: animator, cartoon films. 1925—Married Lillian Bounds. 1928—1st Mickey Mouse. 1933—1st Technicolor-*Flowers & Trees*. 1934—staff of 700 & 1st Donald Duck.

1937—1st full-length animated movie *Snow White and the 7 Dwarfs*. Next 30 years—movies included *Pinocchio* ('39), *Fantasia* ('40), *Bambi* ('43), *Lady & Tramp* ('56), *101 Dalmatians* ('56), + posthumous *The Jungle Book* ('67). Also "True Life Adventures" (animal documentaries)—very popular. + regular movies for children—e.g., *20,000 Leagues Under the Sea*. 1955—Disneyland, CA 1971—Disney World, FL. Died Burbank, CA. Movies still shown regularly—timeless quality, will continue in future.

Exercise 1

Read these notes, and use them to write a short biography.

BRUCE LEE 11/27/40–7/20/73. Real name: Lee Yuen Kam. Born San Francisco, CA. Parents—touring vaudevillians from Hong Kong. Lived in Hong Kong as child. Child actor: 1st film *The Birth of Mankind* ('46) + about 20 other HK film productions. Attended University of Washington, Seattle.1964—Married Linda Emery; 2 children: son, Brandon, born 2/1/65, daughter, Shannon, born 4/16/69. Pursued career in HK and US as martial artist. Taught actors. Developed style of martial arts, Jeet Kune Do. '66–'67: appeared in role of Kato in TV series *The Green Hornet*. Played same role on episodes of TV show *Batman*. Guest roles on other TV shows: *Ironside, Blondie*, and *Here Comes the Bride*. Recurring role of self-defense instructor on *Longstreet*. Appeared in series of kung fu films made in HK: *Fist of Fury* ('71), *The Chinese Connection* ('72), *Enter the Dragon* ('73), *Return of the Dragon* ('73), and *Kato and the Green Hornet* ('74). Considered a cult hero. Died mysteriously in HK while filming a new film. Many films made about him after death. Son Brandon followed in father's footsteps as martial artist and actor. Accidentally shot to death in 1993 while making a film.

continued

Exercise 2

Read these short biographies of Edith Wharton and George Orwell.

Edith Newbold Jones was born in 1862 into a very wealthy and socially prominent New York City family. Though women did not attend school in the 1860s, Edith was privately educated and traveled with her parents in Europe. In 1885, she married Edward Wharton, a Boston banker.

Her first published poetry appeared in 1889 and her first stories a year later. In 1899, a collection of her best stories, *The Greater Inclination*, was published. Her second novel, *The House of Mirth*, was published in 1905, and was a best seller. Wharton wrote frequently about New York high society.

In 1907, Wharton moved to France where she lived the rest of her life. She lived apart from her husband for long periods of time, and their troubled marriage ended in divorce in 1913. During the First World War, she was active in the relief effort for refugees and the children, and was awarded the Legion of Honor by the French government.

Wharton's best known work, the short novel, *Ethan Frome*, was published in 1911. For *The Age of Innocence*, her most sophisticated novel of manners, published in 1920, she won the Pulitzer Prize. A prolific writer, her work included travel books, many articles and reviews, and an autobiography, *A Backward Glance*.

In 1923, Wharton became the first woman to be granted an honorary doctor of letters by Yale University, and in 1930, she became the first woman to receive the gold medal of the National Institute of Arts and Letters. She died in 1937.

Eric Arthur Blair (George Orwell) was born in 1903 in India, where his father worked for the Civil Service. The family moved to England in 1907 and in 1917 Orwell entered Eton, when he contributed regularly to the various college magazines. He left in 1921 and joined the Indian Imperial Police in Burma the following year, in which he served until 1928.

His first published article appeared in *Le Monde* in October 1928, while Orwell was living in Paris, and he returned to England in 1929 to take up work as a private tutor and later as a schoolteacher (1932). *Down and Out in Paris and London* was published in 1933. Due to his poor health, Orwell gave up teaching and worked as a part-time assistant in a Hempstead bookshop, and later was able to earn his living reviewing novels for the *New English Weekly*, a post he kept until 1940.

At the end of 1936 Orwell went to Spain in the Civil War and was wounded. During the Second World War he was a member of the Home Guard and worked for the BBC Eastern Service from 1940 to 1943. As literary editor of *Tribune* he contributed a regular page of political and literary commentary. From 1945 Orwell was the Observer's war correspondent and later became a regular contributor to the *Manchester Evening News*.

Orwell suffered from tuberculosis, and was in and out of hospital from 1947 until his death in 1950. He was forty-six.

His publications include *The Road Wigan Pier*, *Coming Up for Air*, *Keep the Aspridistra Flying* and *Homage to Catalonia*. Orwell's name became widely known with the publication of *Animal Farm* and *Nineteen Eighty-Four*, both of which have sold more than two million copies. All Orwell's works have been published in Penguins.

From the introduction to the Penguin edition of *Down and Out in Paris and London*.

Make notes on Wharton using these headings.

Full name ....

Born (Where? When?) ....

....

Family ....

Early career ....

....

Travel ....

....

Achievements ....

....

....

Interests ....

....

Awards ....

Death ....

Exercise 3

Read the notes on Walt Disney and Bruce Lee.
Make similar notes on George Orwell.

....

....

....

....

....

....

....

Unit 34

Language Summary

If you don't do this, I'll do that.
Unless you do this, I'll do that.

Exercise 1

A Los Angeles baseball team, the Strikers, is about to play the second game of a double-header against the Baltimore Robins. Tommy LoGordo, the Strikers' manager, is very upset about the first game, and he's in the locker room. He's made some notes for his talk to the team.

Unless we win this game, I'll quit.

Write six more sentences.

1. ....

2. ....

3. ....

4. ....

5. ....

6. ....

Exercise 2

If we don't win this game, I'll quit.

Write six more sentences.

1. ....

2. ....

3. ....

4. ....

5. ....

6. ....

LOS ANGELES STRIKERS

1. WIN THIS GAME — OR I QUIT!

2. AVERY (FIRST BASEMAN) — STOP DROPPING THE BALL OR I'LL SEND YOU BACK TO THE MINOR LEAGUES!

3. HODGESON (CATCHER) — STOP ARGUING WITH THE UMPIRE OR HE'LL SEND YOU TO THE SHOWERS.

4. GOMEZ (SHORTSTOP) — PLAY HARDER OR WARM THE BENCH NEXT WEEK.

5. WALKER (PITCHER) — STRIKE OUT SOME BATTERS OR NEVER PLAY FOR ME AGAIN.

6. PINSKI (OUTFIELDER) — PLAY BETTER — OR I'LL PUT IN A SUBSTITUTE.

7. TEAM — START WINNING SOON OR NOBODY WILL PAY TO WATCH US PLAY.

Exercise 3

Put *if* or *unless* into the blanks in these sentences.

1. .... we hurry, we'll miss the bus.

2. Will you call me .... you come to Denver?

3. .... you see Jane, ask her to contact me.

4. You'll never pass your exam .... you don't work harder.

5. The Strikers won't win .... they begin playing better.

6. .... you forget our address, you can find it in the phone book.

7. You won't pass your driving test .... you drive more carefully.

8. He'll get sick .... he doesn't stop worrying so much.

9. We'll go to the beach tomorrow .... it's raining.

10. We'll never get there on time .... the bus leaves soon.

Unit 35

Language Summary

If you did this, I'd do that.
If you did(n't do) this, I would(n't) do that.
Unless you did this, I would(n't) do that.

Look at this:

Exercise 1

I want to see the concert, but I don't have a ticket.
If I had a ticket, I would see the concert.

1. He'd love to see the film, but he's only 13 and he's not with an adult.

....

2. She's almost out of gas. She's got credit cards, but no cash.

....

3. They'd like to rent a car, but he's only 20, and so is she.

....

4. I'd like to borrow some money, but I don't own a house.

....

Exercise 2

Put *if* or *unless* into the blanks in these sentences.

1. I wouldn't buy it .... it had a guarantee.

2. .... I were you, I'd see a doctor about that cough.

3. Who would you ask .... you didn't know how to do it?

4. I'd buy it .... I could afford it.

5. I wouldn't buy it .... I could afford it.

6. I would refuse to go .... they paid my expenses.

7. He's very lazy. He'd pass .... he tried harder.

8. They wouldn't be able to go .... we could find a babysitter.

9. She wouldn't spend all that money .... she weren't very rich.

10. I don't agree with their economic policy. I wouldn't vote for them .... they changed it.

Exercise 3

Justin Shaw is 20. He wants to marry his girlfriend, Noreen, who is 16. He's just been to see her parents, Mr. and Mrs. Casey. This is what Mr. Casey said. "There are just a few conditions, young man. Finish college, get a job, save some money. Find a place to live, sell that noisy motorcycle, stop smoking, stop drinking, cut your hair, remove those tattoos from your arms, and take that earring off. When you've done all these things, we might discuss it again."
They wouldn't let him marry her unless he finished college.

Write nine more sentences with *unless*.

Unit 36

Questionnaire: How Aggressive Are You?

1. **Your car were stuck in a traffic jam, would you:**
   - ☐ **A.** blow your horn, and curse the Mayor and Police Department?
   - ☐ **B.** turn on the car radio, and relax?
   - ☐ **C.** feel slightly annoyed, but resign yourself to the situation?

2. **If you could have a new car, would you prefer to have:**
   - ☐ **A.** a comfortable, luxury sedan?
   - ☐ **B.** an uncomfortable but fast sports car?
   - ☐ **C.** an economical, easy-to-park small car?

3. **If you were watching TV, which of these would you choose:**
   - ☐ **A.** a western
   - ☐ **B.** a romantic comedy
   - ☐ **C.** a boxing match

4. **If you were getting on a bus, and there were only one seat left, would you:**
   - ☐ **A.** rush to get it?
   - ☐ **B.** look to see if there were anyone older who might want it?
   - ☐ **C.** make no special effort to get there first?

5. **If you were at a party and your boyfriend/girlfriend were surrounded by members of the opposite sex who found him/her attractive, would you:**
   - ☐ **A.** grab his/her arm and leave the party?
   - ☐ **B.** feel happy because he/she was having a good time?
   - ☐ **C.** go over, put your arm around him/her and join the conversation?

6. **Do you own any of these (or would like to)?**
   - ☐ **A.** an German Shepherd
   - ☐ **D.** a prize for winning a sports event
   - ☐ **B.** a fast car or motorcycle
   - ☐ **E.** books about war
   - ☐ **C.** a weapon of any kind
   - ☐ **F.** any kind of uniform

7. **A man/woman has killed a child. Should he/she be:**
   - ☐ **A.** put to death?
   - ☐ **B.** imprisoned for life?
   - ☐ **C.** institutionalized for psychiatric treatment?

8. **Have you been in a public argument (or physical fight) during the last two years?**
   - ☐ **A.** often
   - ☐ **B.** once or twice
   - ☐ **C.** never

9. **You have just had an argument with a friend. Would you say:**
   - ☐ **A.** "I won't speak to him/her, unless he/she apologizes to me."
   - ☐ **B.** "I'd better phone him/her and apologize."
   - ☐ **C.** "I think I'll wait and see what happens."

10. **Which of these statements is true for you?**
    - ☐ **A.** "I would never hit anybody unless they hit me first."
    - ☐ **B.** "I would never hit anybody for any reason."
    - ☐ **C.** "I would never hit anybody unless I were very upset."

What did you score?

Results
19–34 You are a fairly aggressive person. I wouldn't want to step on your toes!
7–18   You are a fairly balanced person.
0–6   You may be too calm. Remember that a little aggression is normal.

1. A. 3	B. 0	C. 1	
2. A. 1	B. 3	C. 0	
3. A. 1	B. 0	C. 0	8. A. 3 B. 1 C. 0
4. A. 3	B. 0	C. 0	9. A. 3 B. 0 C. 1
5. A. 3	B. 0	C. 2	10. A. 1 B. 0 C. 4

6. Score 1 for each that you, or would like to have.

Exercise 1

Go through the questionnaire and work out your score.

Exercise 2

Ask another student the questions and work out his/her score.

Exercise 3

If my car were stuck in a traffic jam, I'd be very upset, but I wouldn't blow my horn.

Use your results to write out nine sentences.

Exercise 4

Look at the scores. Do you agree with them? Why/why not? Discuss.

Unit 37

Language Summary

Would you have said anything?
What would you have done?

I	'd	have	said	something.
	would		done	
	wouldn't			anything.

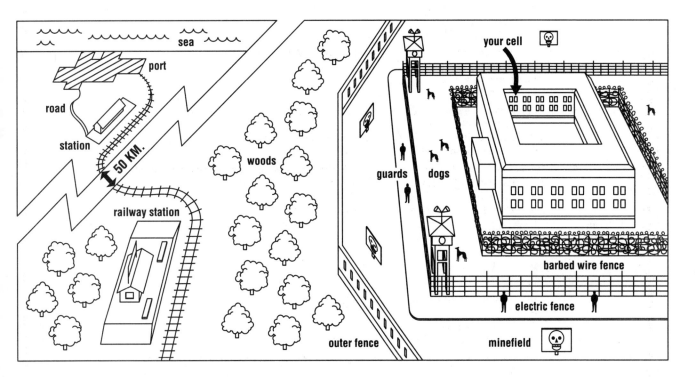

At an army college, student officers were given a problem to solve. They were shown a map of a prisoner-of-war camp. They had to imagine that they were prisoners in the camp. They had some vital information, so it was very important for them to escape. Secret agents couldn't get them out, but they could arrange to leave some things to help the prisoners to escape. The officers had to say how they would have escaped, and what they would have done at each obstacle. Look at the plan of the prison camp, look at the notes, and say what you would have done.

This is what the secret agents provided for the escape.

1. cell, window bars—hacksaw/dynamite.

2. cell to ground—rope/a large balloon.

3. barbed-wire fence—a ladder/wire cutters.

4. dogs—tranquilizers/a knife.

5. electric fence—wire cutters/a shovel.

6. guards—a spare uniform/a gun.

7. minefield—an accurate map/a metal detector.

8. outer fence—a pile of bricks/a long wooden pole.

9. near railway station—a phrase book/a sign saying "deaf & dumb."

10. next station—a car/a bicycle.

11. port—a rowboat/seaman's papers from a neutral country.

Exercise 1

cell, window bars—a hacksaw/dynamite.
I would have used the hacksaw.

Write ten more sentences.

Exercise 2

I would have sawed through the bars.
Write ten more sentences.

Exercise 3

Why wouldn't you have used the dynamite?
Because it would have made too much noise.

Write ten more questions and answers.

Exercise 4

Write a paragraph and describe how you would have escaped and why you would have chosen this method.

Language Summary

If	I he she we you they	'd had hadn't had not	done that, seen that, been there,	I he she we you they	'd would wouldn't would not	've have	done this. seen this. known this.

Look at this:

<table>
<tr><td colspan="4">Lister Hill Hospital
WINFIELD, NC</td></tr>
<tr><td>Emergency Room</td><td colspan="2" align="center">Daily Report</td><td align="right">September 16</td></tr>
<tr><th>PATIENT</th><th>AGE</th><th>INJURY</th><th>CAUSE</th></tr>
<tr><td>Paul Nieves</td><td>2</td><td>minor burns to hands</td><td>fireplace without a screen</td></tr>
<tr><td>Sarah Dean</td><td>4</td><td>scalded face and neck</td><td>pulled pan of boiling water from stove</td></tr>
<tr><td>Mark Goldin</td><td>3 ½</td><td>drank bleach</td><td>not on high shelf</td></tr>
<tr><td>Ernest Smith</td><td>72</td><td>electric shock</td><td>bare wires near plug</td></tr>
<tr><td>Eric Witzler</td><td>48</td><td>broken collarbone</td><td>fell off ladder - nobody holding the bottom</td></tr>
<tr><td>Emma Rodriguez</td><td>10 mos.</td><td>bruises</td><td>fell downstairs - no gate on stairs</td></tr>
<tr><td>Daphne Woods</td><td>31</td><td>deep cuts to arms and legs</td><td>walked through glass door - not safety glass</td></tr>
<tr><td>Claire Lebron</td><td>18 mos.</td><td>ate 20 vitamin pills</td><td>pills not in a childproof bottle</td></tr>
<tr><td>Jason DelVecchio</td><td>5</td><td>cut finger</td><td>mother left scissors on the floor</td></tr>
<tr><td>Florence Chiu</td><td>81</td><td>severe burns</td><td>nightgown caught fire - electric heater near bed</td></tr>
<tr><td>Joseph Korb</td><td>40</td><td>lost half his hair</td><td>hair caught in factory machine - not wearing hat</td></tr>
<tr><td>Ann Blake</td><td>18</td><td>broken leg</td><td>car backed into her - driver didn't look in rearview mirror</td></tr>
<tr><td>David Casey</td><td>26</td><td>broken ribs</td><td>car crashed - had had too much to drink</td></tr>
</table>

Exercise 1

If the fireplace had had a screen, Paul wouldn't have burned his hands.

Write twelve more sentences.

Exercise 2

Look at these newspaper headlines.

The train wouldn't have derailed | *if the engineer had stopped at the signal.*
| *if the engineer hadn't failed to stop at the signal.*

Look at the headlines and write six more sentences.

"Something not going well, Mr. Boxley?"

The novelist looked back at him in thunderous silence.

"I read your letter," said Stahr.

"You've all been very decent, but it's a sort of conspiracy," broke out Boxley. "Those two hacks you've teamed me with listen to what I say, but they spoil it—they seem to have a vocabulary of about a hundred words."

"Why don't you write it yourself?"

"I have. I sent you some."

"But it was just talk, back and forth," said Stahr mildly. "Interesting talk but nothing more."

Now it was all the two ghostly attendants could do to hold Boxley in the deep chair. He struggled to get up; he uttered a single quiet bark which had some relation to laughter but none to amusement, and said, "I don't think you people read things. The men are dueling when the conversation takes place. At the end one of them falls into a well and has to be hauled up in a bucket."

"Would you write that in a book of your own, Mr. Boxley?"

"What? Naturally not."

"You'd consider it too cheap."

"Movie standards are different," said Boxley, hedging.

"Do you ever go to them?"

"No—almost never."

"Isn't it because people are always dueling and falling down wells?"

"Yes—and wearing strained facial expressions and talking incredible and unnatural dialogue."

"Skip the dialogue for a minute," said Stahr. "Granted your dialogue is more graceful than what these hacks can write—that's why we brought you out here. But let's imagine something that isn't either bad dialogue or jumping down a well. Has your office got a stove in it that lights with a match?"

"I think it has," said Boxley stiffly,—"but I never use it."

"Suppose you're in your office. You've been fighting duels or writing all day and you're too tired to fight or write any more. You're

sitting there staring—dull, like we all get sometimes. A pretty stenographer that you've seen before comes into the room and you watch her—idly. She doesn't see you though you're very close to her. She takes off her gloves, opens her purse and dumps it out on a table—"

Stahr stood up, tossing his key-ring on his desk.

"She has two dimes and a nickel—and a cardboard match box. She leaves the nickel on the desk, puts the two dimes back into her purse and takes her black gloves to the stove, opens it and puts them inside. There is one match in the match box and she starts to light it kneeling by the stove. You notice that there's a stiff wind blowing in the window—but just then your telephone rings. The girl picks it up, says hello—listens—and says deliberately into the phone, 'I've never owned a pair of black gloves in my life.' She hangs up, kneels by the stove again, and just as she lights the match, you glance around very suddenly and see that there's another man in the office, watching every move the girl makes—"

Stahr paused. He picked up his keys and put them in his pocket.

"Go on," said Boxley, smiling. "What happens?"

"I don't know," said Stahr. "I was just making pictures."

Boxley felt he was being put in the wrong.

"It's just melodrama," he said.

"Not necessarily," said Stahr. "In any case, nobody has moved violently or talked cheap dialogue or had any facial expression at all. There was only one bad line, and a writer like you could improve it. But you were interested."

"What was the nickel for?" asked Boxley evasively.

"I don't know," said Stahr. Suddenly he laughed. "Oh yes—the nickel was for the movies."

Boxley relaxed, leaned back in his chair and laughed.

"What in hell do you pay me for?" he demanded. "I don't understand the damn stuff."

"You will," said Stahr grinning, "or you wouldn't have asked about the nickel."

man she is looking for. In the meantime, he has fallen in love with

From *The Last Tycoon* by F. Scott Fitzgerald, Charles Scribner's Sons, New York, 1941.

This is a short extract from *The Last Tycoon* by F. Scott Fitzgerald. Fitzgerald was one of the most popular American writers of the 1920s. His career faded in the 1930s and he went to Hollywood to write film scripts. *The Last Tycoon* is his last, unfinished novel. In this scene, George Boxley, an English novelist who is working in Hollywood, goes to see Monroe Stahr, the producer.

Exercise 1

Find words or expressions that mean:

1. 10 cents
2. 5 cents
3. look quickly
4. handbag
5. unbelievable
6. fighting
7. a kind of secret plan
8. people who write only for money
9. ruin something
10. proper
11. avoiding giving a direct yes/no answer
12. a deep hole that is a source of water
13. pulled up
14. throwing
15. put someone to work with
16. let's not discuss [the dialogue]
17. I would agree that ....

Exercise 2

Facial is the adjective from *face*. Write down the adjectives from:

1. nose ....

2. ear ....

3. mouth ....

4. spine ....

Exercise 3

Read the story about the stenographer again.

Why might she have wanted to burn the gloves? What might she have done? Write a paragraph. Say what might happen next and who the man might be.

Unit 40

Language Summary

Unless you'd studied film history, you would never have heard of them.
If only we'd had our grandchildren with us.

Exercise 1

Look at the example, and complete the table.

I'll do it if I have time.	*I would do it if I had time.*	*I would have done it if I had had time.*
If I see her, I'll tell her.	....	....
If she doesn't try, she won't succeed.	....	....
Will you go if I ask you to?	....	....
....	I'd buy it if you gave me a discount.	....
....	....	If I had been ill, I would have stayed at home.
....	If I knew the answer, I would tell him.	....
What will you do if the bus doesn't come?	....	....
....	....	I would have been sorry if she had left.
....	I wouldn't stay in this job if I could find another one.	....
....	They would get wet if it rained.	....
....	....	Would he have passed if he had studied hard?
It won't bite you unless you move.	....	....

continued

....   We wouldn't have gone out unless it
                                                                                                            had stopped snowing.
....

....

....   He wouldn't marry her unless she   ....
                                                       were rich.
....

Will you pay him if he does the job?   ....

                                        ....

Exercise 2

Complete these sentences

1. He wouldn't have jumped if ....

2. You'll never learn English unless ....

3. If you don't stop smoking, ...

4. If you go to the casino, ...

5. If I were the mayor, ...

6. If I could go anywhere in the world, ...

7. I would never forgive you if ....

8. If I'd seen the price tag, ...

9. I wouldn't have lent him the money if ....

10. If you don't practice, ...

11. I'll kill you if ....

12. Unless it's a nice day, ...

13. She wouldn't have bought it unless ....

14. If he'd known the police car was behind him, ...

15. She wouldn't have married him unless ....

16. You would earn more money if ....

17. I wouldn't go unless ....

18. I wouldn't have believed him if ....

19. If I had a three-month vacation ....

20. I wouldn't have done this exercise unless ....

Review

Read through Units 1–40 in the Student Book, and answer these questions.

Unit

1. What does Ron Eng do? ....

2. What will William Paine be doing at 8 o'clock? ....

3. Where and when was Paine born? ....

4. How far will each competitor have driven by Friday night? ....

5. What is Roxanne tired of doing? ....

6. What do you send with your résumé to a potential employer? ....

7. What has the Housing Authority promised to give Mrs. Hamilton? ....

8. Why did Reggie send a sympathy card to Jim? ....

9. What does Barbara always have to remind Jonathan to do? ....

10. What does Zach want for lunch? What does Chloe want for dinner? ....

11. Why does Wendy ask to take off next Friday? ....

12. Why will James need some small change? ....

13. Where is James's driver's license? ....

14. What's a loony? ....

15. What is Lynn Bunker interested in buying? ....

16. How did Cobb get burned? ....

17. What brand of jeans is Carla looking for? ....

18. What are three alternative energy sources for cars? ....

19. What was the cause of the food poisoning? ....

20. Why did Steve offer so much money for the painting? ....

21. What does Harriet think Howard might be doing in the backyard? ....

22. What was Terri supposed to be doing? ....

23. What did she pretend to do after the woman took a second doughnut? ....

24. Why was J.D. arrested last year? ....

25. Who do you think killed Mr. Tifton? ....

26. What is Stuart Amos upset about? ....

27. What should the customer have read? ....

28. What cargo was the Mary Celeste carrying to Genoa? ....

29. Why does Mark say, "They must have been eating"? ....

30. What was the name of Marilyn Monroe's last film? ....

31. What did Alex apologize for doing? ....

32. What did Mr. Estrella stop to do on Boyle Street? ....

33. What was the Beatles' most famous album? ....

34. What will happen to the swimmer unless he turns around? ....

35. Terry wouldn't take the job in Mandanga unless she were offered four things. What are they? ....

36. What percent of Alaska is covered by glaciers and ice fields? ....

37. What would you have done if you had been in Jane Dare's situation? ....

38. What might have happened if Rob hadn't noticed Tim's mistake? ....

39. What color are Edward's eyes and hair? ....

40. What does Florence think is a "must" for anyone with kids? ....